# 10

# MINUTE GUIDE TO

# TRAVEL PLANNING ON THE NET

by Thomas Pack

## que®

A Division of Macmillan Computer Publishing
201 West 103rd St., Indianapolis, Indiana 46290 USA

*For my wife, Debbie, who has traveled the world, and for my daughter, Larissa whose adventures have just begun.*

## ©1996 Que® Corporation

Library of Congress Catalog Card Number: 97-65529

International Standard Book Number: 0-7897-1218-0

99  98  97     8  7  6  5  4  3  2  1

Interpretation of the printing code: the rightmost double-digit number is the year of the book's first printing; the rightmost single-digit number is the number of the book's printing. For example, a printing code of 97-1 shows that this copy of the book was printed during the first printing of the book in 1997.

*Printed in the United States of America*

**Publisher** Roland Elgey

**Vice President and Publisher** Don Fowley

**Publishing Manager** Joe Wikert

**Editorial Services Director** Elizabeth Keaffaber

**Managing Editor** Thomas Hayes

**Acquisitions Editor** Martha O'Sullivan

**Technical Specialist** Nadeem Muhammed

**Product Development Specialist** Melanie Palaisa

**Production Editor** Kathryn Purdum

**Acquisitions Coordinator** Michelle Newcomb

**Book Designer** Barbara Kordesh

**Cover Designer** Dan Armstrong

**Production Team** Angela Calvert, Dan Caparo, Mary Hunt, Beth Rago

**Indexer** Robert Long

*Special thanks to Bill Bruns for ensuring the technical accuracy of this book.*

# CONTENTS

# Introduction

## Exploring the Net Can Help You Explore the World

Technological developments often have led to revolutions in travel and tourism. The development of the jet engine, for example, made the world seem smaller not only because it made remote places more accessible, but also because it made international travel, which had been the province of the rich, more affordable.

Now the world is shrinking again because of another technology: the Internet. It empowers people to explore our planet as never before. Information on destinations, advice on how to get there, and tools that facilitate the journey are at the fingertips of anyone who has Internet access.

This book shows you how to use those online travel tools and information resources. It will be useful for business travelers, parents planning family vacations, campers, honeymooners, golfers, skiers, and even armchair adventurers who want to take virtual vacations.

So whether you want to travel by land, sea, air, or modem, this book will show you how traveling the Net can help you travel the world.

## What Type of Resources Are Available?

The Internet can put you in touch with online reservations systems, tour operators, currency converters, air-fare bargains, weather forecasts, foreign language lessons, massive databases of information on countries, cities, restaurants, hotels, entertainment, attractions — and that's just a sampling.

Why is so much travel-related information available online? Because travel and tourism are multitrillion-dollar industries. Companies involved in them believe the Internet represents not only a new way to compete with other companies but also a new way to connect with customers worldwide.

That means a lot of basic travel information on the Web is free; companies offer gratis information in hopes of getting you to visit their sites and eventually buy their products or services.

Government agencies also publish a lot of travel information on the Internet because tourism is an important part of most economies. It's the first, second, or third most important industry in nearly every area of the U.S. It's a primary source of revenue in several other countries, and it represents the largest portion of money spent in international commerce.

You may encounter one difficulty in using online travel resources: They change very quickly. As some observers have noted, three months equals about one year on the Internet. Web sites remodel their interfaces. New companies, services, products, and technologies seem to appear daily. Others disappear without warning.

Whenever possible, this books focuses on Internet resources created by established companies, government agencies, and other types of reliable organizations. But there are no guarantees, and the inclusion of any site in this book is not necessarily an endorsement of its products or services.

As a general rule, approach information on the Internet with caution. Lesson 1 notes that the Net combines some of the best attributes of other types of electronic media and communications technology, but the Net also includes some of the worst aspects. For example, you may come across sales pitches from unscrupulous people and companies. If you feel at all uncomfortable about the legitimacy of the people or company sponsoring an Internet site, don't do business on it or transmit personal information to it.

Fortunately, most Web sites are reliable and genuinely helpful. Several different types of sites are especially useful for travelers:

- **Transactional sites**—Many sites let you use online reservation systems that are Web-based versions of the same systems travel agencies use. Some sites also let you perform transactions such as ordering travel supplies or camping equipment.

- **Databases**—Many sites include large collections of information about countries, cities, restaurants, hotels, and transportation providers.

- **Search engines**—These let you search through millions of Web pages to find sites with information on particular topics, sites from certain companies, and other specific types of information.

- **Directories**—Some sites are basically guides to other sites.

- **Electronic publications**—The Web provides electronic versions of traditional travel publications as well as digital magazines that exist only online.

- **News services**—These can provide details on current travel and tourism stories.

With so much travel information available online, you may want to make it a habit to hit the Net before you hit the road.

## How to Use This Ten Minute Guide

This guide provides step-by-step lessons designed to introduce you to the variety of travel resources available online. Some lessons guide you through directories and databases that can help you find the information you're looking for. Other lessons explain tools such as travel planning programs or currency converters. Several lessons focus on resources for specific types of travelers. All the lessons are designed to give you the skills you need to access travel information in ten minutes or fewer.

If you're new to the online world, start with Lesson 1. It explains the Internet, the Web, and helps you choose an Internet service provider. You then may want to continue through the book lesson-by-lesson to master the basics of many different types of travel planning. Or you may want to jump around in the book and explore only the lessons focusing on the specific types of information you're interested in. You may even want to ignore the step-by-step lessons and use this book simply as a directory to some of the best online travel resources.

## Conventions Used in This Book

To help you move quickly and easily through the lessons, this guide uses several standard conventions. For example:

- Text displayed on your computer screen is printed in **bold** type.

- Buttons, icons, menu items, and text you click appears in color type.

- Text you type onto the screen is printed in **bold color** type.

You also will find important notes set off from the main text in boxes such as these:

**Plain English**   These boxes explain new or technical terms.

**Timesaver Tips**   These boxes highlight shortcuts or other quick ways to get a job done.

**Panic Button**   These boxes warn you of potential problems and offer solutions.

## A NOTE ABOUT TRADEMARKS

Trademarks, service marks, and other corporate property mentioned in this book are indicated by appropriate capitalization (for example, Microsoft Internet Explorer, Netscape Navigator, America Online).

Every effort has been made to ensure the accuracy of this information. If there is any inappropriate capitalization or spelling, it has no effect on the ownership or validity of a trademark or service mark. Also please note that all the Web pages shown in this book are the property of their publishers.

All terms mentioned in this book that are known to be trademarks have been appropriately capitalized. Que cannot attest to the accuracy of this information. Use of a term in this book should not be regarded as affecting the validity of any trademark or service mark.

# Understanding the Net

*In this lesson, you'll learn the basics of the Internet and find tips on choosing an access provider.*

## What Is the Internet? What Is the Web?

On one level, the Internet is simply a network of computer networks. On another level, it is much more. It's perhaps the most powerful information technology ever developed.

Yes, the Net has been hyped in the mass media, but the digital revolution is real. The Internet combines vast collections of information with a worldwide communication system and some of the best features of other media, including magazines, books, television, radio, and movies.

The Internet offers so much information because it links tens of millions of computers in companies, educational institutions, non-profit organizations, and government agencies worldwide. You can become part of the network through your own computer. When you do, you can access the information collections and online services created by others.

The World Wide Web (also called the Web or WWW) is the multimedia part of the Internet. Organizations and individuals publish "pages" on the Web. Pages can contain text, photos, maps, diagrams, audio, video, and links to software programs or other pages. Web publishers organize collections of pages and make them available through a single Web site.

**Web Page**   A single document on the Web. It can contain text, images, audio, and links to other pages.

**Web Site**   A collection of Web pages developed and maintained by an organization or an individual.

Besides the Web, there are many other facets to the Net, including:

- **Gopher**   An Internet protocol that lets people browse databases and transfer files through sites on the Internet. It's named after the mascot at the University of Minnesota, where it was developed.

- **File Transfer Protocol (FTP)**   A method of sending and receiving computer programs and other types of files between computers on the Internet.

- **Newsgroups**   Electronic message boards that let you read comments from others and post your own.

These are areas you may want to explore in depth as you begin to understand the Internet, but this book primarily focuses on Web sites. They often offer the best and the easiest to use travel resources. You will find details on newsgroups in Lesson 15, "Participating in Travel Newsgroups."

## Getting on the Net

What do you need to access the Internet? BaBasically, you need a computer, a fast modem, a phone line, Internet software, and an account with an online service or an Internet Service Provider.

Many machines on the market now—everything from televisions to hand-held devices—promise to let you link to the Internet, but to take advantage of everything the Net offers, you still need a powerful computer, especially if you want to store and process the information you find.

A modem (derived from modulator/demodulator) translates analog signals of the telephone system into digital pulses your computer can understand. Modem speed is measured in bits per second (bps). To use the Web, you need at least a 14,400 bps modem. But that's a bare minimum. Moving around the Web at that speed can be very slow going, especially when you're accessing Web pages with a lot of images or other types of multimedia elements—and travel sites often have these elements. As a rule of thumb, get the fastest modem you can afford.

If you spend a lot of time online, you may want to consider installing a special type of telephone line called ISDN (integrated services digital network). It increases your access speed up to 128,000 bps. The downside is that your phone company will charge you premium prices to install and operate an ISDN line. In addition, you'll need a special ISDN modem.

## BROWSING THE WEB

You can get the software you need to access the Internet from your service provider (described in the next section). An important part of the software is called a Web browser.

The most popular browsers are Netscape Navigator and Microsoft Internet Explorer (see Figure 1.1). Both are powerful browsers with similar features and functions, including the ability to connect with Web pages, move back and forth between them, download and save information, and make secure transactions (for example, transactions that provide protection for personal information such as credit card numbers).

Online services such as America Online, CompuServe, and the Microsoft Network include a browser as part of the software you use to access their services. Many online services also let you use one of the more popular browsers. Figure 1.2 shows America Online's version of Netscape Navigator.

FIGURE 1.1 Microsoft's Internet Explorer is a popular and powerful Web browser.

When you first connect to the Internet through your browser, the page you see is called a *home page*. It usually is a page maintained by your Internet provider. Many providers let you customize this page so it presents the information you want every time you connect.

You can visit other Web sites by entering an address in the browser's location box, located at the top of the large window in which you view Web pages. A Web site address is called an URL (Uniform Resource Locator). The acronym is pronounced "Earl." An URL tells your browser where to find the site you're looking for. URLs start with the letters **http**, which stands for HyperText Transfer Protocol (for example, the URL for The New York Times is http://www.nytimes.com).

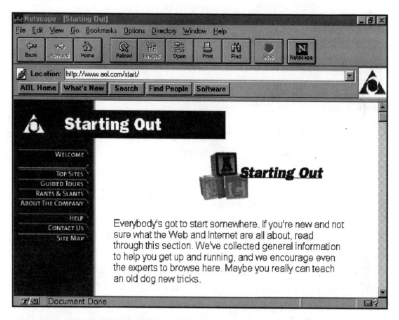

**FIGURE 1.2**    America Online offers subscribers a customized version of Netscape Navigator.

**Omitting the http://**    Many Web browsers will insert the http:// part of a Web URL for you, so you can omit it when you enter the address—www.nytimes.com, for example.

You also can visit other sites and pages on the Web simply by pointing with your cursor and clicking with your mouse. The items you point and click include buttons, icons, and highlighted text, which represent *links* (sometimes called hyperlinks or hypertext) to other pages, either within the Web site you're visiting or to a completely different site. You can tell when your cursor is pointing at link because it changes from an arrow into a pointing finger.

# CHOOSING AN INTERNET PROVIDER

To get started on the Web, you need to establish an account with an online service or an Internet Service Provider (also known as an ISP).

Online services include:

**America Online** (1-800-827-6364)

**CompuServe** (1-800-848-8990)

**Prodigy** (1-800-213-0992)

**The Microsoft Network** (1-800-386-5550)

All these services provide Internet access as well as their own well organized collections of online information, including a great deal of travel information (Lesson 25, "Finding Travel Information on America Online," provides an overview of that service's features). Most online services offer several different pricing plans, including "fee-plus" accounts, which charge a predetermined fee for a few hours of usage per month—usually about $10 for five hours. You'll pay between $2.00 and $2.50 for each additional hour.

Some ISPs operate on a national level and sign up members from all over the country. These include:

**SpryNet** (1-206-957-8998)

**IBM Internet Connection Service** (1-800-821-4612)

**Concentric Network** (1-800-745-2747)

**IDT Internet Services** (1-201-883-2000)

**Whole Earth Networks** (1-415-281-6500)

Other ISPs operate on a local level. Look for them in your yellow pages under Internet Service Providers. If you travel a lot, a national provider may be your best choice so you can get connected when you're on the road.

Many telephone companies have entered the ISP business, too. For example, AT&T Worldnet Service (1-800-400-1447) and MCI Internet (1-800-550-0930).

In the past, online services have been easier to set up and use than ISPs, but online services usually were more expensive because of their per-hour charges. ISPs also have tended to offer more powerful Web browsers and other Internet access tools, including e-mail, newsgroup, and chat applications.

Today, the differences between online services and ISPs are becoming less discernible. Most online services now provide powerful Internet access tools, and many are offering flat-rate pricing plans that provide unlimited access for a fixed fee of about twenty dollars per month. That's the same rate most ISPs charge (though some have indicated they may not be able to continue offering unlimited access at that price much longer). A flat-fee plan usually is your best value if you spend more than about fifteen hours online every month.

Most online services and ISPs offer free trial periods you can use to explore their services without incurring online charges. Take advantage of this time to try before you buy. Here are some evaluation tips:

- Make sure the provider lets you access the Internet through a local dial-up number or a toll-free 800 number. You don't want to pay long-distance phone charges in addition to online fees.

- Make sure the provider has an adequate number of technical support and customer service representatives. If you have to wait an extremely long time on a support line, you should choose another provider.

- Make sure the provider's technicians can explain answers to your questions in terms you can understand. If you need assistance installing your software or learning how to use it, the technicians should be ready, willing, and able to help.

- Make sure the provider has sufficient bandwidth, which means they should have the technological ability to handle a lot of online traffic without causing you to receive busy signals, slowdowns, or access problems. Ask the provider about its subscriber to modem ratio. Anything higher than 10:1 is too high. You should be warned, however, that some slowdowns on the Web are inevitable, especially during peak hours when most people use the system. However, if you consistently encounter slowdowns or access difficulties, the problems may lie with the service provider.

To help you compare providers, you can access a Web site called The Ultimate Guide to Internet Service Providers (see Figure 1.3). It offers reviews of ISPs and ranks them according to ratings submitted by Internet users who have registered to become members of CNET, the site's sponsor. You don't have to be a member to read the reviews.

Of course, you do need Internet access before you can search the site. If you don't have it yet, perhaps you can perform this lesson on the computer of a friend or colleague who does. If you already have a provider, this lesson may help you determine how other services compare to yours.

Searching the site is a good test of your provider's Internet resources, so you may want to make it one of your first online journeys during your free trial period.

To find information at the Ultimate Guide to Internet Service Providers:

1. Type the URL **http://www.cnet.com/Content/ Reviews/Compare/ISP/** into your Web browser's location box and press **Enter**.

2. When the welcome screen appears, scroll down and click the text that says **Top National ISPs** (see Figure 1.3).

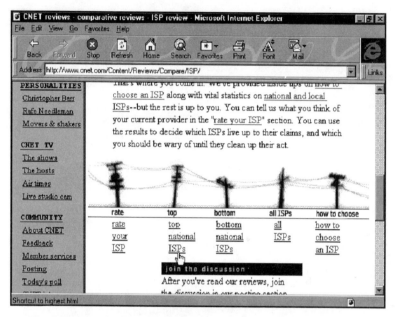

**FIGURE 1.3** The Ultimate Guide to Internet Service Providers offers extensive reviews and ratings.

3. On the next page, scroll down to the list of ISPs. Reviews are available for the ones that have stars next to their names.

4. To read a review, click the ISP's name. If you click a name without a star, your browser will take you to the provider's Web site. After you read a review or visit a site, you can use the **Back** button on your browser to return to the list of top ISPs.

5. If you want to find information on ISPs in your area, click the button labeled **All ISPs** beneath the list of Top ISPs.

6. Scroll down the All ISPs page and click the button labeled **Search by area(s) served** (see Figure 1.4).

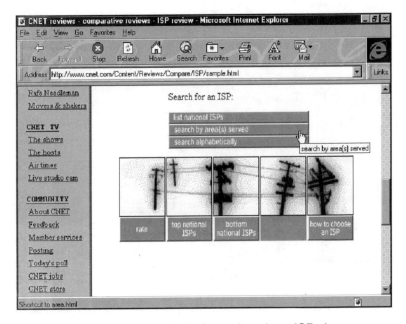

**FIGURE 1.4**    Click here to find information about ISPs in your state.

7. Select your state from the list in the box. Then click the **Submit** button.

8. Like the list of Top ISPs, the list of local providers offers reviews for services with stars next to their names. If you click on the name of an ISP without a star, your browser will take you to the ISP's site.

Other Web sites that may help you find ISPs include:

- The List (**http://www.thelist.com**) provides information on ISPs around the world. For the U.S. and Canada, you can also search by state or province.

- The Web directory Yahoo! offers links to U.S., regional, and international ISPs. The site also provides a directory of other ISP directories. To use Yahoo!, use the URL

**http://www.yahoo.com**, and then select the following categories and subcategories: Business and Economy, Companies, Internet Services, Internet Access Providers.

# USING THE INTERNET CONNECTION WIZARD

Miscrosoft's Internet Connection Wizard offers an easy way to get on the Internet. It provides access to worldwide Internet Service Providers through a centralized service, and it offers detailed instructions throughout the sign-up process.

The wizard is included with later releases of Windows 95 and Internet Explorer as well as the Microsoft Plus! Windows add-on program. To see if you have the wizard on your computer, search for the file Inetwiz.exe. You may be able to run it by clicking the **Start** button and then selecting **Programs**, **Accessories**, **Internet Tools**, and **Get on the Internet**.

If you don't have the program, you can download the latest version of Microsoft Internet Explorer from **http://www .microsoft.com/ie/download/**.

When you run the Internet Connection Wizard, it will walk you through the process of getting on the Net step-by-step. You can use the program to set up a connection through a regular phone line or a local area network.

# WEB SITES FOR INTERNET NEWCOMERS

Several Web sites provide information that's especially useful for people new to the Net:

- Yahoo! Internet Life Surf School: **http://www.zdnet .com/yil/filters/surfjump.html**
- Global Village Tour of the Internet: **http://www .globalvillage.com/gcweb/tour.html**

- Newbie.Net Cyber Course: **http://www.newbie.net/ CyberCourse/**

- Matt's Five-Minute Guide to the Internet: **http://www. iquest.net/~mjdecap/beginner.htm**

Yahoo! also offers links to many more newcomer sites. Go to the home page (**http://www.yahoo.com**) and then select the following categories: Computers and Internet, Internet, Information and Documentation, Beginner's Guides.

QUE, the publisher of this book, also offers several printed beginner guides. For more information, visit the QUE site at **http:// www.mcp.com/que**.

In this lesson you learned Internet basics and found tips on choosing an access provider. In the next lesson, you'll learn how to protect yourself from computer viruses.

# Protecting Yourself Against Viruses

*In this lesson, you'll learn how to download anti-virus software and track virus information.*

## What Are Computer Viruses?

There are more than 10,000 known computer viruses. At least six new ones are created or modified from old ones every day.

What are they? They're pieces of software that get into your machine without your knowledge or permission. Some viruses are designed to activate relatively harmless programs that just display messages or play music. Others viruses can cripple your computer. They can corrupt programs, or even erase your hard drive.

Viruses get into a computer through a segment of software code that implants itself in an executable file and then spreads from one file to another. You cannot get a virus simply by using the Internet or browsing the Web. You can get viruses from some types of e-mail attachments and from infected programs you download from the Net or an online service. Most online services scan their file libraries for viruses. Most Internet sites are safe, too. But you can't be too safe when it comes to viruses.

Still, only about 40 percent of computer users have anti-virus programs, according to the National Computer Security Association (**http://www.ncsa.com**), a Carlisle, Pennsylvania organization that certifies anti-virus software. NCSA also reports that many people install protective software only after they become infected.

You can help protect yourself before you have a problem by staying up-to-date on virus information and by downloading anti-virus software from the Internet.

# Finding Virus Information on the Web

Here's a sampling of sites that provide basic virus information, anti-virus programs, or both:

- AntiVirus Resources: (**http://www.hitchhikers.net/ av.shtml**) offers extensive news, alerts, basic information, and software. You can register for automatic e-mail notification of software upgrades.

- Symantec Antivirus ResourceCenter: (**http://www. symantec.com/avcenter/index.html**) provides alerts and a virus information database (part of the site's Home Page is shown in Figure 2.1). You also can purchase and download copies of the popular programs Norton Anti-Virus or Symantec AntiVirus for Macintosh (but you may get them cheaper from a mail-order company or software retail store).

- IBM AntiVirus: (**http://www.av.ibm.com/current/ FrontPage/**) offers virus and hype alerts as well as advice for people who think their computers are infected. You also can find a large collection of detailed technical information.

 **Virus Hype and Hoaxes**   Sometimes Internet pranksters spread dire warnings of impending virus plagues. These false alarms won't hurt your computer, but they can waste your time. Web resources such as the IBM site mentioned above provide information that can help you debunk virus hype. Another site you may want to visit is Computer Virus Myths (**http://www.kumite.com/myths**).

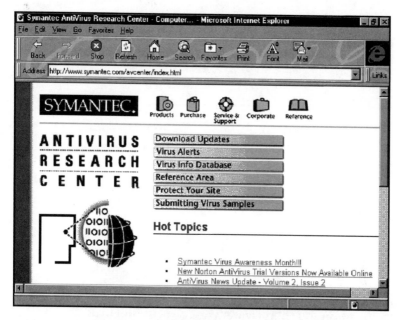

FIGURE 2.1 Symantec offers several resources that can help you protect yourself from viruses.

- Virus:Information: (**http://csrc.ncsl.nist.gov/virus/**) provides reviews of anti-virus software and miscellaneous information from the National Institute of Standards and Technology's Computer Security Research Clearinghouse.

- The Computer Virus Help Desk: (**http://www. indyweb.net/~cvhd**) offers basic information and an extensive selection of links to other virus sites.

- Stiller Research: (**http://www.stiller.com**) provides lengthy, but easy-to-understand basic information on viruses. You also can download a shareware version of the Integrity Master anti-virus program.

**Shareware** This is software you can use and evaluate before you decide to buy it. The program will contain information on how to pay for and register it if you decide to keep it.

- McAfee: (**http://www.mcafee.com**) provides a Virus Info Library, downloadable software, and a unique feature called SecureCast. It will automatically send you regular updates of anti-virus technology. SecureCast is free to any McAfee customer.

- Dr. Solomon's: (**http://www.drsolomon.com**) offers Virus Alerts, a searchable Virus Encyclopedia, a full tutorial, help with virus infections, details on hoaxes, and information on several anti-virus software programs.

You can find many other anti-virus sites through a list of links at the NCSA site (**http://www.ncsa.com/hotlinks/ virus.html**).

## DOWNLOADING ANTI-VIRUS SOFTWARE

The Dr. Solomon's site mentioned in the previous section provides information on anti-virus programs for DOS, Windows 3.x, Windows 95, Windows NT, NetWare, OS/2, Macintosh, and SCO UNIX. You can find out where to buy the programs at the site. You also can download a free evaluation version of FindVirus for DOS. Here's how:

1. Type the URL http://www.drsolomon.com/ in your Web browser's location box and press Enter.

2. Scroll down Dr. Solomon's Home Page and click the Download icon (see Figure 2.2).

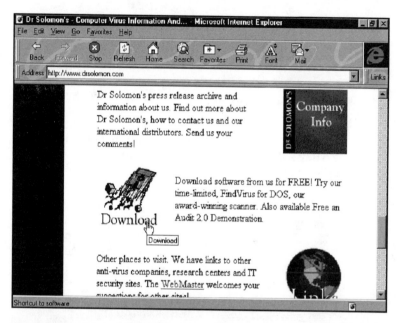

**FIGURE 2.2** You can download a free anti-virus program at Dr. Solomon's.

3. On the next page, click the link FindVirus For DOS v7.68 1.2MB. Please note that this page also offers links to information on software products for other computer platforms, and you download a free Virus Tutorial.

4. The next page provides basic information about FindVirus and an online registration form. After you've filled it out, click the Submit button near the bottom of the page.

5. The next page lets you choose either a "lite" or standard version of FindVirus. Click the name of the one you want in the appropriate geographic category for your location.

6. Your Web browser may display a dialog box asking whether you want to save the file or open it with a helper application. Choose Save.

7. Your browser then will display a box asking where you want to store the file. Select one of your existing folders, or create a new one.

8. The program is delivered as a compressed file. You'll need to open it with file decompression software (see the following note).

9. After you've decompressed the FindVirus, read the text files. They will help you install, set up, and use the program.

**Compressed File**   A file that has been reduced in size so you can download it quickly is referred to as a compressed file. Some online services (America Online, for example) provide built-in programs that automatically decompress files after you download them. If the Internet software you use doesn't offer that feature, you can use decompression software such as WinZip for PCs or Stuffit for Macs. WinZip is available at **http://www.winzip.com**; **Stuffit**, and at **http://www.aladdinsys.com**.

To find out where to buy other Dr. Solomon programs, click the Company Info icon on the site's home page (you can return to it by using the Back button on your browser). On the Company Info page, scroll down and click the Contacting Us link. Then click US/ UK resellers and distributors. When you select the link for your geographic location, you'll receive a list of Dr. Solomon's vendors. Click a vendors name for more information and a link to its Web site.

## MONITORING VIRUS INFORMATION WITH ONLINE SERVICES

Most online services offer their own areas that can help you track virus information and download software. America Online, for example, offers both a PC Virus Information Center (keyword:

**pc virus**) and a Macintosh Virus Information center (keyword: **mac virus**). Both offer virus news, message boards, real-time chat sessions, and libraries of anti-virus programs (see Figure 2.3).

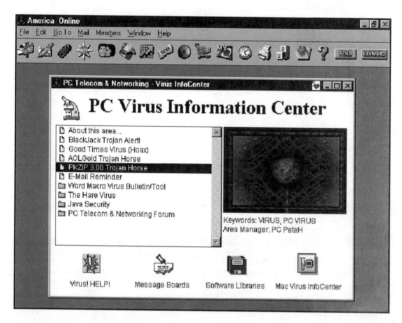

**FIGURE 2.3** Most online services offer virus information for their members. For example, America Online's PC Virus Information Center can help you learn how to stay protected.

In this lesson, you learned how to protect yourself from computer viruses. In the next lesson, you'll learn how to use online travel planning resources.

# 3

# USING TRAVEL PLANNING RESOURCES

*In this lesson, you'll learn how to create a custom travel guide. You'll also learn where to find other travel tools and software on the Web.*

## CREATING YOUR OWN GUIDEBOOK

Fodor's, the largest publisher of English-language travel guides, sponsors a Web site that offers a special feature called Personal Trip Planner. You can use it to create a customized travel miniguide to large cities across the U.S. and around the world. You also can create miniguides for several island destinations (for example, Bermuda, Puerto Rico, Jamaica, and the U.S. Virgin Islands).

To use the Personal Travel Planner:

1. Type the URL **http://www.fodors.com** in your Web browser's location box and press Enter.

2. On Fodor's Home Page, click the Personal Trip Planner link (see Figure 3.1).

3. On the next page, select a destination from the list in the scrollbox. In Figure 3.2, the traveler has selected Bermuda. (If the place you're most interested in isn't listed, don't worry. You'll learn how to find information on many other places in Lesson 7, "Finding Destination Information.")

4. On the same Web page, you can customize your guide by clicking the appropriate boxes for information on hotels, restaurants, recommended activities, and travel tips.

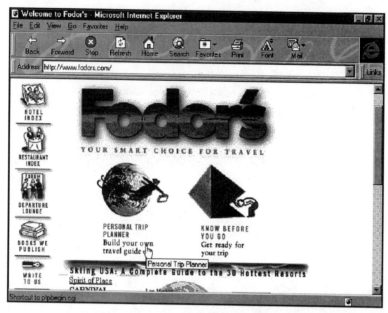

**FIGURE 3.1**  Fodor's is a Web site sponsored by the leading travel guide publisher.

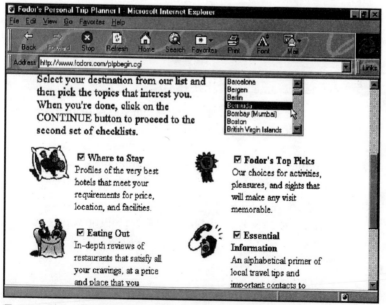

**FIGURE 3.2**  Fodor's lets you create a personalized travel guide.

5. Click the Continue button near the bottom of the page
   (not shown in Figure 3.2). Please note that it may take
   Fodor's a few minutes to process your request.

6. On the next Web page, click the appropriate checkboxes
   to include hotel and restaurant price ranges as well as
   local travel tips and advice. Figure 3.3 shows the type of
   tips you can choose from.

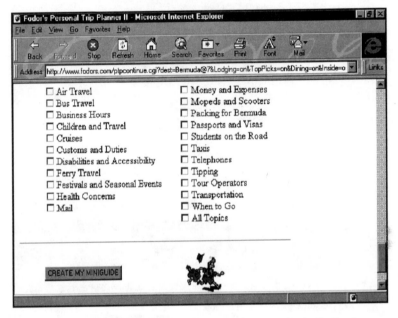

**FIGURE 3.3**    The Personal Trip Planner lets you specify the types
of destination information you want.

7. After you make your selections, click the button labeled
   Create My Miniguide.

8. Fodor's will present basic information on your destination (see Figure 3.4) as well as details on all the topics you
   selected.

**Save It!**  If you create a miniguide you want to keep, check out Lesson 4 to learn how to save information you find on the Web.

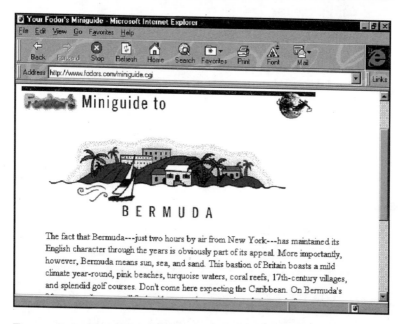

**FIGURE 3.4**  Your Miniguide will include basic information on your destination as well as all the other details you selected.

# FODOR'S OTHER PLANNING FEATURES

Fodor's site offers many other useful features to help you plan your trip. On the home page you can find links to travel articles, information on Fodor's books, and hotel and restaurant indexes.

Fodor's Departure Lounge (refer to Figure 3.1) is a forum for travelers to post messages. You can ask for advice on an upcoming trip and share stories about the adventures you've already taken.

In Fodor's Know Before You Go section (see Figure 3.1), you can find travel planning tips and links to other useful sites. Know Before You Go is divided into several subsections:

- **Focus on Photography**
- **Language for Travelers**
- **Smart Travel Tips**
- **Currency Converter**
- **World Weather**
- **Free Travel Services**
- **Government Travel Advisories**
- **Government Health Advisories**
- **U.S. Yellow Pages**

Additional information on most of the above topics is available in other lessons in this book.

# More Travel Planning Tools and Software

Here are the addresses of several other travel planning resources on the Web. Some of them provide general planning tools; others are designed for specific types of travel planning (golf trips, for example).

- Europe by Eurail (**http://www.eurail.com/**) lets you download a free copy of EuroData, a European trip planning program. You also can find information on European Rail Passes and even order them online.

- Epicurious Travel (**http://travel.epicurious.com/**), the online home of *Conde Nast Traveler* magazine, offers a Planning Section with a hyperlinked traveler's checklist.

- MaxMiles (**http://www.maxmiles.com/**) offers frequent flyer software.

- CD-ROM Travel Planners (**http://www.cdromtravel .com**) sells electronic travel guides focusing on resorts, hotels, golf, tennis, skiing, hunting, fishing, hotels, and bed and breakfast inns.

- Personal Passport (**http://www.personalpassport.com/**) lets you order a multimedia CD-ROM with travel information from more than 1,200 companies, including cruise lines, tour companies, airlines, and hotels.

- TravRoute Software (**http://www.travroute.com/**) sells Road Trips Door-to-Door, a program that can help you generate detailed driving instructions (see also Lesson 11, "Generating Online Maps").

- Rand McNally Online (**http://www.randmcnally.com**) offers information on the TripMaker CD-ROM. It combines an electronic Road Atlas and trip planning software. Rand McNally also offers an online database of information on road construction. You can use it directly through the Web site's travel tools section.

- DeLorme (**http://www.delorme.com**) sells several digital map products, including AAA Map'n'Go, which helps you find the fastest, shortest, or most scenic route to a destination. The software also offers complete AAA TourBook information. You can order the products and get updates from the Web site. DeLorme also offers an online version of the Map'n'Go technology. You can use the online CyberRouter (**http://route.delorme.com/**) to generate maps and driving instructions between more than 240,000 places in the U.S. The CyberRouter page also includes a link to a CyberAtlas (if you're interested in online maps, see also Lesson 11).

- GoldenWare Travel Technologies (**http://www2. traveldesk.com**) offers a travel planning program called Electronic Travel Desk. You can download a free copy from the site.

- U.S. Golf Packages (**http://www.golftravelplus
  .com/**) offers information on a software program called
  GOLFTRAVELplus.

In this lesson, you learned about travel software and online planning tools. In the next lesson, you'll learn how to save information from the Net onto your own computer.

# Saving the Information You Find

*In this lesson, you'll learn how save text, images, and documents you find on the Internet.*

## Saving Text Files

If you find a Web page with valuable information, how do you save it so you can refer to it later?

This lesson illustrates how to save a Web page as a plain text ASCII file you can open in your word processor. You will not save any formatting or graphics from the page. In Internet Explorer, the graphics will be replaced with the word "picture," which you can, in most cases, easily delete from the file. Occasionally, you may come across a page that is virtually unreadable when you save it as a text file.

To save all the text on a Web page:

1. Click File on your Web browser's menu bar.

2. Click Save As (in Netscape) or Save As File (in Microsoft Internet Explorer—see Figure 4.1).

3. A dialog box will open and ask where you want to save the file. Select a folder or create a new one.

4. In the File name box, type a name for the page.

5. Make sure you're saving the file as a text file and not as an HTML file (see the definition below). In Internet Explorer, click the box at the bottom of the dialog box and change it to read Save as Type: Plain Text (see Figure 4.2). In Netscape Navigator you can use Save File as Type: All Files if you add the **.txt** extension (for example, **Bermuda.txt**).

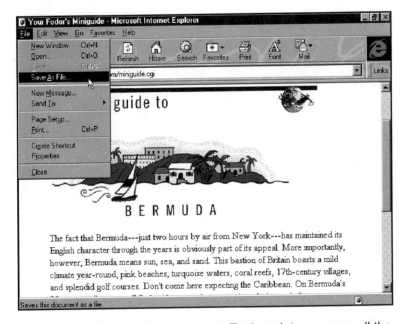

**FIGURE 4.1**    Save As File in Internet Explorer lets you save all the text on a Web page.

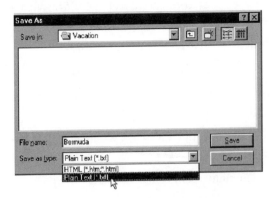

**FIGURE 4.2**    Make sure you save the Web page as a text file.

6. Click Save or OK, depending on your browser. This will save the file as a plain text ASCII file.

**HTML**   HyperText Markup Language is the page format used to make up the Web itself. When people create Web pages, they format plain ASCII text with HTML tags, which are codes that tell your Web browser how to display the text on a page.

**TIP**

**Curious about HTML Codes?**   If you want to see how Web publishers have created files, use the file extension .htm or .html instead of .txt in the above lesson. After you save and open the file in your word processing program, you will see the HTML coding. An even quicker way to see it when you're visiting a Web page is to select Source from your browser's View menu.

# SAVING EXCERPTS FROM WEB PAGES

Sometimes you may not want to save every bit of text on a page. As noted above, many pages will have extraneous information on them when they're saved as text files, and some pages, like the Bermuda miniguide, can be very long.

To copy an excerpt from a page, and then paste it in a word processing document:

1. Select the information you want to copy by clicking the Web page at the beginning of the text and dragging to highlight all the text you want to copy. Figure 4.3 shows part of the Bermuda miniguide has been highlighted.

2. In your Web browser, click the Edit menu, or the right button on your mouse. Then click Copy.

3. Open the word processing document where you want to put the information.

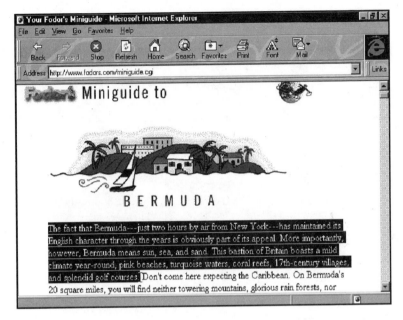

**FIGURE 4.3** Highlighting text lets you save excerpts from Web pages.

4. Click the location in the document where you want to place the excerpt. Open the Edit menu and choose the Paste command. The text from the Web page will appear in your document.

**Text You Can't Save** Sometimes text on a Web page actually is part of an image. This often is true of text in logos, icons, and section headings. That type of text cannot be saved by either method illustrated above. With the second method, you can identify text that won't be copied because you won't be able to highlight it with your cursor.

# SAVING IMAGES

Besides text, most Web browsers now offer an easy way to save images. Here's how:

1. Position your pointer over the image.

2. Click your right mouse button or, if you're a Mac user, hold the mouse button down.

3. A menu will pop up. Select Save This Image As or Save Picture as.

4. A dialog box will appear. Choose a directory, a name for the file, and a graphic format such as **.bmp** (see below). Then click Save.

**bmp** This is a popular format for graphic files. Derived from BitMaP, the format can handle 16.7 million colors and often is used for Windows wallpaper. You also can open bmp files in the Windows Paint program. Another popular format is **GIF** (Graphics Interchange Format). It creates smaller files than bmp, but it is a low-resolution format that supports only 256 colors. If you really want to get involved with digital images, you need a software program that will let you view and manipulate different formats. LView Pro, for example, is a shareware image file editor for Windows. You can download a copy from http://world.std.com/~mmedia/lviewp.html. You can find other programs for Windows or Mac at CNET's Shareware.Com (**http://www.shareware.com/**).

# A NOTE ABOUT COPYRIGHT

Most organizations with Web pages do not mind if you copy text or images for your own personal use. If you copy them for any other purpose, most organizations mind very much—and you may be violating copyright law. Sometimes Web developers publish their copyright policies online. If you can't find them and you're uncertain about whether or not you can legally copy part of a Web page, follow the general rule professional researchers have followed for years: When in doubt, get permission.

# Downloading PDF Documents

Some Web sites let you download and save documents in prepared formats. The Portable Document Format (PDF) is one of the most popular and useful. For example, you can download passport applications in the PDF format (see Lesson 8, "Using Government Sources of Travel Information"). You also can download PDF maps of Disney World (see Lesson 20, "Visiting Amusement Parks"). Because PDF is an easy-to-use format that handles both text and graphics, expect many travel sites to offer PDF documents soon.

PDF is easy-to-use because it is device- and application-independent. That means they can be viewed and printed from any computer—as long as you have the Acrobat Reader software from Adobe Systems, Inc. installed on your computer. To download a free copy of Acrobat Reader:

1. Type the URL **http://www.adobe.com/** in your Web browser's location box and press Enter.

2. Scroll down Adobe's Home Page and click the button labeled Get Adobe Reader.

3. In Adobe's downloading section, click the highlighted word registering in step one (see Figure 4.4).

4. On the registration form, Adobe requires you to enter at least your name and mailing address. After you type the information into the form, click the button labeled Submit Registration.

5. Your Web browser will take you back to the screen shown in Figure 4.4. Choose a computer platform and language from the pop-up lists.

6. Click the OK button near the bottom of the page.

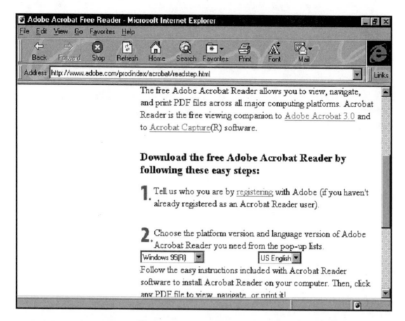

The free Adobe Acrobat Reader allows you to view, navigate, and print PDF files across all major computing platforms. Acrobat Reader is the free viewing companion to Adobe Acrobat 3.0 and to Acrobat Capture(R) software.

**Download the free Adobe Acrobat Reader by following these easy steps:**

**1.** Tell us who you are by registering with Adobe (if you haven't already registered as an Acrobat Reader user).

**2.** Choose the platform version and language version of Adobe Acrobat Reader you need from the pop-up lists.

Windows 95(R)          US English

Follow the easy instructions included with Acrobat Reader software to install Acrobat Reader on your computer. Then, click any PDF file to view, navigate, or print it!

**FIGURE 4.4**   Downloading a copy of the Adobe Acrobat Reader is free and easy.

7. On the download page, click the DOWNLOAD via HTTP link.

8. Your browser may open a dialog box asking if you want to save the file or open it with a helper application. Select Save.

9. Your browser will open another box that asks where you want to put the file. Select a directory or create a new one.

10. When the download is complete, quit your Web browser, run the program you just downloaded, and follow the simple installation instructions on your screen. After you've installed the program, you can point and click to download PDF documents whenever you're on the Web. Adobe Acrobat Reader will launch automatically and load the PDF file.

**Don't Close the Installer**    If there's a technical problem or interruption while you're downloading the Adobe Acrobat Reader, the installer application will perform a complete uninstall. Therefore, you shouldn't close the program at the end of the download. It may not be completely finished. Just wait a few seconds and it will close automatically.

In this lesson, you learned how to save information you find on the Internet. In the next lesson, you'll learn how to use Web search engines.

# SEARCHING THE WEB WITH SEARCH ENGINES

*In this lesson, you'll learn how to use online resources that can help you find Web sites with information on specific topics.*

## WHAT ARE SEARCH ENGINES?

Browsing the Web involves jumping from one site to another and following links that look like they'll provide further information on topics of interest.

Searching the Web involves looking for a specific site or a specific type of information. How can you find it among the millions of pages on the Web?

You use search engines. They're based on a technology that continually scans the Internet and indexes sites, pages, and other types of information. The search engines described in this lesson do not focus solely on travel information, but they're presented here for two reasons:

- They can help you find travel information (or any other type of information) not mentioned in this book.

- Once you understand the basics of using search engines, you'll be able to use similar techniques to search the databases at many other sites, including some that have databases of travel information.

When you use a search engine, you enter keywords in a search entry box. The engine then generates a list of "hits" that provide links to the Internet information containing your keywords. Most search engines are supported by online advertising, so using them is free.

**Keywords**   Keywords are words or phrases describing the information you want to find. They can be the names of companies, people, or subject terms such as "travel agencies" and "cruise lines."

**Hits**   These are items in your search results list that were retrieved by your keywords. When you're using search engines, hits usually are links to other sites. If you're searching a database of documents—magazine articles, for example—hits would refer to the articles your keywords retrieved.

## A SAMPLE SEARCH WITH EXCITE

Excite is a search engine that helps you find information in more than fifty million Web pages. Like most other search engines on the Web, Excite will look for documents containing exact matches to the keywords you enter, but Excite goes further and automatically looks for documents containing synonyms and concepts related to your keywords.

To begin an Excite search:

1. Type the URL **http://www.excite.com** in your Web browser's location box and press Enter.

2. When Excite's Web page appears on your screen, type **keywords** in the search entry box and click the Search button. In Figure 5.1, the user has entered the keywords **ski trips**. Note that you do not have to enter punctuation or grammatical sentences. If you're using Excite to look up a proper name such as Colorado or Aspen Ski Tours, just capitalize the first letters of each word as you normally would. Excite will find only the Web pages containing the terms as proper names.

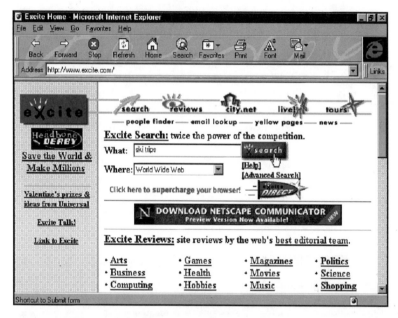

**FIGURE 5.1**   Excite is a search engine that can help you find information in more than fifty million Web pages.

3. When the results page appears, scroll through the list. You will see a list of hits, which are links to many different types of Web pages. The percentage sign next to each hit is a *confidence rating*. You'll notice some of the sites are relevant to the information you're looking for, several sites may be only somewhat relevant, and many will not even be close (see Figure 5.2).

**Confidence Rating**   The percentage sign next to each hit is a confidence rating. The closer the rating is to 100 percent, the more confident Excite is that the hit is the type of information you want.

4. When you see a hit that looks interesting, click the highlighted words. Your Web browser will take you to that site.

**5.** After you visit a site, click the Back button on your Web browser to return to the Excite search engine. You then can evaluate other sites through other links.

**6.** When you find a site you like, use your Back button to return to Excite and then click the text next to the site's link that says More Like This (see Figure 5.2). Excite then will generate a new list of hits that should include more links relevant to your topic. Excite initially presents search results sorted by relevance, which is indicated by the percentage rating. If you want your search results to be organized by the sites with the most pages containing your keywords, click the Sort by Site button near the top of the results page.

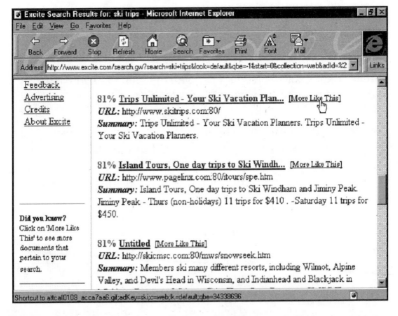

**FIGURE 5.2**  When you find a site you like, click [More Like This] to create a new list of hits.

## A Sample Search with AltaVista

Another powerful search site you may want to use is AltaVista. It indexes more than thirty million Web pages. It offers both simple and advanced search engines. To use the simple engine, just enter your keywords in the search entry box on AltaVista's Home Page (**http://www.altavista.digital.com**).

Here are tips for using the simple search engine:

- If you want to search a multi-word phrase, put it in quotation marks. For example, if you put the phrase **"ski trips"** in quotation marks, you'll ensure that those two words appear together in the Web pages you're seeking.

- Capitalize proper nouns as you did in Excite.

- AltaVista ranks your search results so that the Web pages containing the most keywords are listed first.

- AltaVista doesn't index punctuation, so don't include it in your search.

At this writing, AltaVista is developing a new feature designed to help you refine a simple search. LiveTopics will analyze the contents of documents that meet your original search criteria, and then display groups of related words you can choose to include in the search. Run a simple search through AltaVista to find the latest information on the availability and functionality of LiveTopics.

# Using Advanced Search Techniques

Having too much information can be as bad as having no information. When you're using a search engine, how can you enhance your search results to increase the number of relevant hits while decreasing the number of false hits?

Instead of entering just simple keywords in a search engine, you can use keywords with *Boolean* and *proximity operators*. You also may want to use wildcard characters. Don't let those terms scare you. Sophisticated search techniques sound more complicated than they are. And once you know how to use them, you'll realize they're worth the little extra effort they require.

## USING BOOLEAN OPERATORS

Boolean operators are named after the English mathematician George Boole (1815-1864) because they reflect his work in mathematical logic. Sometimes they are called logical operators. They include **AND**, **OR**, and **NOT**. You can use them to broaden or narrow the scope of your search because they specify the logical relationships between your keywords.

- The **AND** operator narrows a search because it indicates that two or more keywords must be found in the same Web page. For example, if you enter **ski** and **trips**, you're telling the search engine that both **ski** and **trips** must appear on the pages you want the engine to find for you.

- The **OR** operator broadens a search because it indicates that either keyword must be in a page. If you enter **ski or snowboard**, you're telling the search engine to find pages containing either **ski** or **snowboard** or both.

- The **NOT** operator, sometimes expressed as **AND NOT**, narrows a search because it indicates that a keyword must not appear on the pages you want to find. If you enter **ski NOT clubs**, you're telling the search engine that you want pages with the word **ski** on them but you don't want them if they also have the word **clubs**.

These are simple examples, but Boolean operators can help you create complex, precise search strategies—especially on systems that also let you use parentheses to group keywords. For example, you could create a strategy that looks similar to this:

(ski or snowboard) AND (trips OR vacations OR tours) AND NOT clubs.

What does that mean in regular English? You're telling the search engine that the Internet pages or documents you want to find must contain either the word **ski** or **snowboard**. They also must have either the word **trips** or **vacations** or **tours**. But they cannot contain the word **clubs**.

The Boolean search shown above is a generic example. It will work in both AltaVista's advanced interface (explained below) and in Excite, but it won't work in all Web search engines because not all of them let you use advanced search techniques. The Web search engines that do work may process them in different ways, or substitute different operators for the ones explained here (such as, using a minus sign instead of the NOT operator).

To learn how to use advanced techniques for any search engine, spend a few minutes in the site's help files. You'll find that it's a good investment of your time because advanced techniques will reduce the amount of irrelevant information you retrieve. In fact, it's a good idea to look for tips in the help files of any search engine you're using even if you're doing only simple searches.

## USING PROXIMITY OPERATORS

Proximity operators let you specify how close one of your keywords should be to another in the Web pages you're trying to find.

The most common proximity operator used by Web search engines is **NEAR**, which tells the system that you want one keyword to be within a certain number of words of the other. For example, if you enter **ski NEAR trips**, you're telling the search engine that you want **ski** and **trips** to be within X words of each other. Some search engines let you determine the value for X. Other systems interpret **NEAR** to mean within a value set by the search engine.

Other proximity operators you may be able to use include **WITH**, **ADJ** (short for adjacent), and **FOLLOWED BY**. All these operators tell the search engine that your first keyword must immediately precede the one that follows it (for example, **ski with trips**).

## USING WILDCARD CHARACTERS

Wildcard characters help you find plurals and alternate spellings of your keywords because they let you specify that a letter in a word can be replaced by any other letter or by none at all. For example, if you use the common wildcard character * at the end of the word **ski***, you'll retrieve Internet pages with both the singular and plural forms of the word. You also will retrieve pages with the word **skiing**.

If you use a wildcard in the middle of the word **organi*ations** you'll retrieve Internet information with the English spelling **organisations** as well as the American spelling **organizations**.

## ADVANCED SEARCHING WITH ALTAVISTA

AltaVista is a search engine that lets you use wildcard characters and Boolean and proximity operators.

To begin an AltaVista search:

1. Type the URL **http://www.altavista.digital.com/** in your Web browser and press Enter.

2. Click the Advanced button at the top of AltaVista's main screen.

3. In the Selection Criteria window, enter a search statement that includes some of the advanced techniques explained in this chapter. In Figure 5.3, the traveler has entered **(ski* or snowboard*) near (trip* or tour* or vacation* or adventure*).** AltaVista interprets NEAR to mean within ten words. If you need to use Boolean operators as keywords, put them in quotation marks (for example, **"and"**). To help rank your search results, enter keywords in the Results Ranking Criteria window. In the above example, the traveler has entered **ski* snowboard*.**

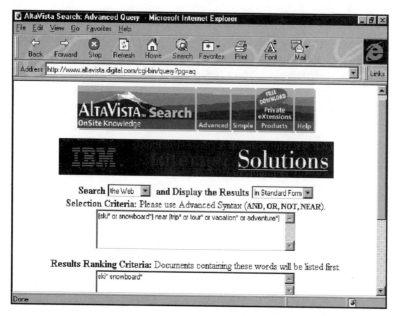

**FIGURE 5.3** AltaVista lets you use many advanced search techniques.

**4.** After you have filled in both windows, click the Submit Advanced Query button (not shown in figure 5.3). You can leave the Start Date and End Date windows empty.

When you receive the search results list, compare it with the one you created with Excite. Because you used advanced techniques that offer more precise searching, AltaVista will create a smaller set of results, but they should be, on average, more relevant (see Figure 5.4).

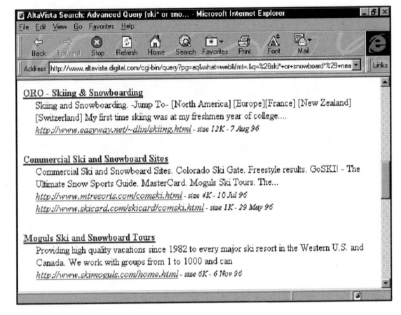

FIGURE 5.4    When you use advanced search techniques, you can produce highly targeted search results.

# USING OTHER SEARCH ENGINES

No single search engine will meet all information needs. Here are notes on several other sites you may want to try.

- HotBot (**http://www.hotbot.com**) indexes more than fifty-four million Web sites as well as content in newsgroups.

- Infoseek (**http://www.infoseek.com**) helps you search through more than 1.5 million Web sites as well as newsgroups, company directory listings, e-mail addresses, and Web FAQs (answers to Frequently Asked Questions).

- Lycos (**http://www.lycos.com**) covers sixty-six million sites. Besides text, you also can search the Web for images and sound files.

- Magellan (**http://www.mckinley.com**) includes numerous categories and subcategories. Magellan also offers a directory of rated and reviewed sites.

- Webcrawler (**http://www.webcrawler.com**) indexes about two million sites. It also offers an extensive selection of Web site reviews.

- Yahoo! (**http://www.yahoo.com**) categorizes about 400,000 sites. Because they are indexed by humans instead of automated technology, you usually will find many high-quality links. (You'll use Yahoo! in Lesson 6. It is also mentioned in several other lessons because it's an excellent directory to many different types of travel information.)

**Search Engine Limitations**  Web search engines do not index pages that require the user to enter a password. That's why you can't find information from, say, newspaper articles available through *The New York Times* site. You can access them directly through the site: **http://www.nytimes.com/**.

## SPECIALIZED SEARCH ENGINES

- MetaCrawler (**http://www.metacrawler.com**) is a metasearch site. That means it lets you perform one search through several other engines at the same time. MetaCrawler helps you search through nine sites, including Excite, Lycos, and WebCrawler.

- Four11 (**http://www.four11.com**) is a White Pages service, which means it helps you find contact information for people. Use 411 to find e-mail addresses and telephone numbers.

- DejaNews (**http://www.dejanews.com**) searches more than 20,000 newsgroups. (For more information about them, see Lesson 15, "Participating in Travel Newsgroups.")

In this lesson, you learned how to use Web search engines. In the next lesson, you'll learn how to use directories and databases of travel information.

# 6

# USING TRANSPORTATION AND TRAVEL DIRECTORIES

*In this lesson, you'll learn about directories of travel information.*

## FINDING INFORMATION ON PLANES, TRAINS, CRUISES, AND MORE

The last lesson focused on resources that can help you find all types of information on the Internet. This lesson focuses on digital directories and databases designed especially to help you find travel-related sites on the Web.

One such resource is Reed Traveler.Net, sponsored by Reed Travel Group, a member of the Reed Elsevier plc group and one of the world's largest suppliers of travel information products (see Figure 6.1).

Traveler.Net offers several travel directories and databases. Travel Weekly Online, for example, contains about 1,000 links to sites in such categories as Air Travel, Cars, Cruises, Railroads, Theme Travel, Tours, and Agencies. The directory is updated twice weekly.

Travel Weekly Online is easy to use:

1. Type the URL **http://www.traveler.net** in your Web browser's location box and press Enter.

2. On Traveler.Net's Home Page, click the button labeled Travel Weekly Online (see Figure 6.1).

**FIGURE 6.1**  Traveler.Net can help you find other travel sites on the Web.

3. The next page you see will show the categories you can research (see Figure 6.2). Select one by clicking either its button or the text underneath the button.

4. Some of the categories offer a "Quick 'n' Chunky AlphaIndex" that can help you search through the list quickly. For example, in the Tours category you can click the letter E or O at the top of the page to jump to that part of the list.

5. Each category offers links to some of the Net's top travel resources. To visit one of the sites in the list, just click its name. After you visit another site, if you want to return to Travel Weekly Online, use the Back button on your Web browser.

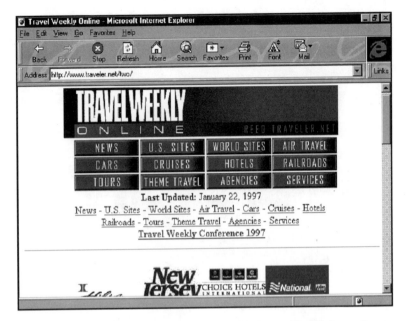

**FIGURE 6.2** Travel Weekly Online can help you find information on cars, trains, planes, cruises, tours, and much more.

# OTHER TRAVELER.NET FEATURES

Travel Weekly Online is just one of the useful features you'll find at Traveler.Net. Look for these other services on the Traveler.Net Home Page:

- **ABC Corporate Services**—This service offers information on Internet services and corporate discounts on business travel.

- **HotelBook by Utell International**—This is a free gateway to reservation services for more than 6,500 hotels worldwide.

- **Hotel & Travel Index Online**—This feature provides a directory of links to thousands of hotels on the Web. You can also read hotel reviews sponsored by the Official Hotel Guide.

- **Meetings & Conventions Online**—Use this resource for meeting planners. (If you're interested in meetings and conventions, see Lesson 17, "Using Business Travel Resources.")

- **OAG Online**—This one offers a selection of airport time-tables, airline schedules, and information on hundreds of cities around the world.

- **Reed Travel Group**—This service provides basic information on the group, its divisions, and career opportunities.

# USING YAHOO!

To access the travel directory at Yahoo!:

1. Type the URL **http://www.yahoo.com** in your Web browser's location box and press Enter.

2. On Yahoo's home page, click the word Travel under the Recreation and Sports category.

3. Near the top of the next page, you'll see that you can search the Yahoo! travel section with keywords (see Figure 6.3). For best results, use quotation marks around multi-word phrases (**"American Airlines"** for example). For advanced search options and tips, click the word Options.

4. If you click the word Regions beneath the search entry window, you can access links to tourism offices, online tour guides, and other types of destination information for states, countries, and continents. As shown in Figure 6.3, the text near the top of the page also lets you access travel-related events on the Net, an online reservation service, and a directory of other travel directories.

5. Scroll down the page and you can find links to travel information in more than 20 categories (see Figure 6.4). Just click the name of the category for the type of information you're interested in.

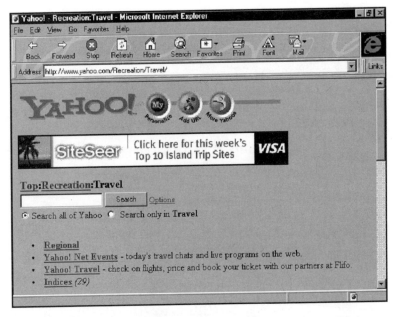

**FIGURE 6.3**  Yahoo! lets you search its collection of travel links.

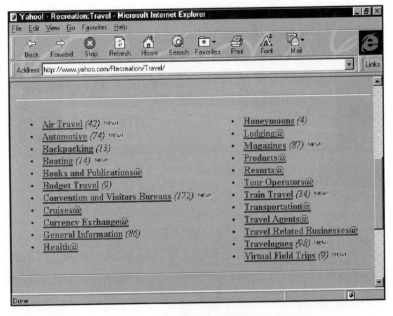

**FIGURE 6.4**  Find links to travel information in more than 20 catagories.

The @ symbol at the end of a category means that the heading is listed in multiple places within Yahoo!. You can click the heading to go to the primary location. For example, if you click the Travel Related Businesses@ heading, you'll see lists of companies involved in the travel industry, including airlines, boat charter services, limousines, passport services, and many others. You also can access a directory to 60 other travel company directories.

# OTHER ONLINE DIRECTORIES

Here's a sampling of other electronic travel directories you can search on the Web. These are general directories that cover several different types of travel resources. Many other lessons in this book offer information on specialized travel directories. For example, you'll find details on camping directories in Lesson 21, "Camping in Cyberspace."

- EarthLink, a Web site hosting service, offers a travel section (**http://www.earthlink.net/travel/**) that can help you find sites in such categories as Resources, Destinations, Thematic Travel, and Virtual Travel.

- InfoHub WWW Travel Guide (**http://www.infohub.com/**) offers information on transportation, destinations, special interest travel, accommodations, and traveler assistance.

- TravelLinks (**http://www.trvltips.com/travellinks.html**), sponsored by *TravelTips* magazine, offers information in such categories as Agencies, Destinations, Ezines (electronic magazines) & Resources, Lodging, Services, Shopping, Sports Travel, and Transport.

- The Web Surfers Travel Guide (**http://pages.prodigy.com/JohnnyO/**) covers everything from airlines to weather.

- Travel.org (**http://www.travel.net**) offers information on trips, agents, airlines, lodging, and countries.

- Travel Solutions (**http://www.travelsolutions.com**) provides collections of links in such categories as Airlines, Airports, & Charters; Automobiles, Limos, Taxis & RVs; Food and Fun; Trains, Subways & Ferries; and Travel Opportunities for Students.

In this lesson, you learned how to use online travel directories. In the next lesson, you'll learn how to find information on destinations.

# FINDING DESTINATION INFORMATION

*In this lesson, you'll learn how to find information on countries and cities.*

## FINDING COUNTRY INFORMATION

The *World Travel Guide* has been recognized as one of the best destination guides ever published. The World Travel Guide On-line, a joint venture between Columbus Press and AT&T, combines the editorial excellence of the printed guide with the power of electronic information technology. The result is a Web site that lets you quickly and easily find detailed information on any country in the world.

The heart of the World Travel Guide Online is the A to Z Country Fact Finder. Here's how to use it:

1. Type the URL **http://www.wtgonline.com** in your Web browser's location box and press Enter.

2. On the World Travel Guide's Home Page, click the globe icon under the words Click Here.

3. The next page lets you use an interactive map or an alphabetical index to find information on a specific country (see Figure 7.1).

4. Choose a country in one of the following ways:

    • Click the map and select from a list of countries in the continent you clicked.

    • Click a letter in the index and select from a list of countries beginning with that letter.

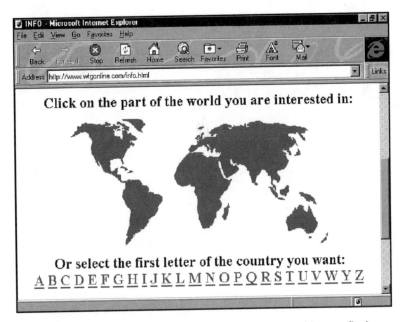

**FIGURE 7.1** The A to Z Country Fact Finder can help you find information on any country in the world.

5. You'll receive a page with basic information such as population, geography, history, language, and government. Click the circular icons to receive additional information (see Figure 7.2). You also can view online maps for many countries.

Besides the Fact Finder, the World Travel Guide Online offers an extensive selection of links to other Web sites focusing on specific geographic regions. You can browse them by clicking the word Links in the menu bar on the Travel Guide's Home Page. The site also offers a hotel finder you can search through a simple keyword interface.

**FIGURE 7.2**    The A to Z Country Fact Finder offers highly detailed information.

# FINDING CITY INFORMATION

City.Net, a special feature of the Excite search engine described in Lesson 5, "Searching the Web with Search Engines," offers detailed information on cities as well as restaurants, attractions, and art and entertainment venues.

To use City.Net:

1. Type the URL **http://city.net** in your Web browser's location box and press Enter.

2. On City.Net's Home Page, there are different ways to find information on a specific destination. You can:

    - Scroll to the bottom of the page and click a name in the list of Top 25 U.S. Cities or the list of Top 25

International Cities. Top cities are determined by the number of times City.Net users have retrieved information on them.

- Search City.Net through the search engine in the middle of the page. (In Figure 7.3, the user has entered the destination **Key West**.)

3. Your search results will include links to several relevant Web sites, including city guides (for example, Discover Key West), lodging directories (for example, Aaron's Hotel & Motel Catalog for Key West), and weather sites.

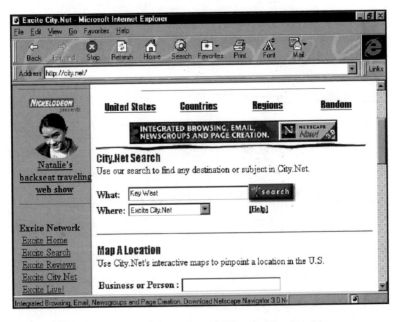

**FIGURE 7.3**    City.Net offers detailed information on cities worldwide.

Other features available through City.Net include Maps and a Concierge service. The map feature lets you pan across cities, zoom in to street level, and pinpoint a street address. You even can print maps on your own printer. (City.Net's maps are supplied by MapQuest, a Web site explained in detail in Lesson 11, "Generating Online Maps.")

The Concierge feature offers links to various online directories, including those covering art, entertainment, restaurants, hotels, transportation, and weather.

You can access the Maps and the Concierge feature at the top of City.Net's Home Page. You also can access information on countries and continents by clicking either the word Countries or the word Regions near the top of the page.

# USING ELECTRONIC YELLOW PAGES

If you click the text that says Yellow Pages on any City.Net page, you'll have access to BigBook, one of the many electronic phone directories available on the Web.

**TIP**  **Shortcut**   You can access BigBook directly with the URL **http://www.bigbook.com**.

Electronic yellow pages can help you search specific cities for addresses and phone numbers of hotels, restaurants, transportation services, shopping centers, and other types of businesses that may be of interest to travelers.

The online phone directory called Zip2 (**http://www.zip2. com**) lets you search for those businesses through a simple keyword interface or an interactive map (see Figure 7.4).

If you're looking for businesses around the world, try the electronic yellow pages at ComFind (**http://www.comfind.com/**). If you want to try even more yellow pages, look through Yahoo! Use the URL **http://www.yahoo.com** and then select the following categories: Reference, Phone Numbers, Businesses. If you want to find Web sites with electronic white pages, which

can help you find the names and addresses of people, choose the
Yahoo! categories Reference, Phone Numbers, Individuals.

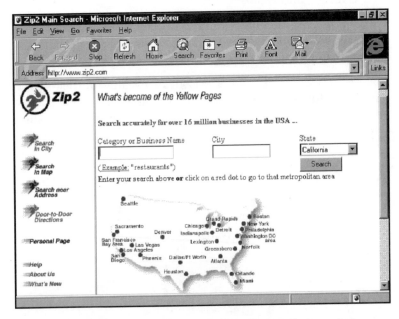

FIGURE 7.4    Zip2 is an electronic Yellow Pages that can help you
find listings for millions of U.S. businesses.

## OTHER SOURCES OF DESTINATION INFORMATION

Here are the addresses of several other Web sites that can provide
information on cities and countries:

- TravelCOM (**http://www.travelcom.es**) offers the
  Worldwide Travel Index. It provides links to country information through an interactive world map.

- eGO Travel (**http://www.ego.net/**) offers information
  through an interactive map of the U.S. You also can find
  travel tips, news, and travelogues.

- Open World's City Guides (**http://www.openworld. co.uk/cityguides/**) is a project in progress that plans to offer comprehensive information on 100 of the most visited cities worldwide.

- Open World also offers Welcome to Britain (**http:// www.openworld.co.uk/britain/**), which features information on hotels; heritage attractions; theatres; museums; restaurants; and shops in England, Scotland, and Wales.

- Travelocity (**http://www.travelocity.com**), an online reservation system, offers a Destinations & Interests section with extensive information on cities around the world. You can find details on art exhibits, children's activities, festivals, tours, lodging, museums, performing arts, sports, restaurants, shopping, and wilderness areas. You can search the Destinations & Interests section with keywords.

- Microsoft's Expedia offers the World Guide, an illustrated electronic guidebook to more than 250 destinations. A special feature provides 360° panoramic photos online. Expedia also offers a hotel directory with 25,000 entries (see Lesson 9, "Booking Travel Online," for more information about Expedia).

Many of the directories explained in Lesson 6 also offer links to destination information.

In this lesson, you learned how to find destination information. In the next lesson, you'll learn how to use online information from government sources.

# USING GOVERNMENT SOURCES OF TRAVEL INFORMATION

*In this lesson, you'll learn how to find passport and visa information, travel and health advisories, and contact information for tourism offices.*

## FINDING PASSPORT AND VISA INFORMATION

The U.S. Department of State's Bureau of Consular Affairs offers a great deal of valuable information for people traveling abroad. For example, you can find detailed passport and visa information. You even can download a passport application directly to your computer. Here's how:

1. Type the URL **http://travel.state.gov** in your Web browser's location box and press Enter.

2. Scroll down the Bureau of Consular Affairs home page and click the text that says Passport Information.

3. Scroll down the next page and click the text that says Download Printable Passport Applications (see Figure 8.1).

4. On the next page you'll see information on the type of paper you need to print the application. You'll also see that the forms are available in the PDF format explained in Lesson 4, "Saving the Information You Find."

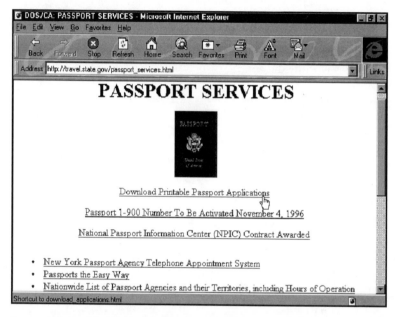

**FIGURE 8.1**    You can get passport applications directly from the Web.

**Adobe Acrobat Reader**    If you didn't download a copy of the Adobe Acrobat Reader in Lesson 6, you can do it now directly from the passport services page. Just click the text that says Click here for more information and to download Adobe Acrobat Reader free of charge.

5. If you already have the Adobe Acrobat Reader, select the text that says Click here to select the forms to download.

6. The next page will provide information on choosing and submitting the forms. To download the form you need, just click its name and it will be transferred to your computer in the PDF format.

If you need to learn about visas, click the words Visa Information on the Bureau of Consular Affairs' Home Page. You then can browse through a list of links to basic information. If you click the link that says Foreign Entry Requirements (look under the Visa Publications heading), you'll find a list of visa requirements for countries worldwide.

**TIP**   **Searching an Individual Web Page**   The Foreign Entry Requirements page is a very long document with a lot of text on it. That's not a problem if you're going to Argentina, but what if your destination is Zimbabwe? Do you need to scroll all the way to the bottom of the page? Probably not. Most Web browsers provide an easy way to find individual words on Web pages. Just click Edit on the browser's menu bar and then click the text that says Find on This Page. A window will open, and you can type in the word or phrase you want to find on the Web page you're viewing. If you search for the word **Zimbabwe**, for example, your browser will jump to the first mention of it on the page.

# MONITORING TRAVEL ADVISORIES

To find travel advisories, select the text that says Travel Warnings/ Consular Info Sheets on the Bureau of Consular Affairs Home Page. You then will see the page pictured in part in Figure 8.2. (You can access this page directly from anywhere on the Internet with the URL **http://travel.state.gov/travel_warnings. html.**)

As you scroll the travel advisories page, you'll find various types of information, including:

- **Travel Warnings**—These are issued when the State Department decides to recommend that Americans avoid travel to a certain country.

- **Consular Information Sheets**—Available for every country of the world, these sheets include such information as location of the U.S. Embassy or Consulate, unusual immigration practices, health conditions, minor political disturbances, unusual currency and entry regulations, crime and security details, drug penalties, and information on any unstable condition not severe enough to warrant a Travel Warning.

- **Public Announcements**—These offer information on terrorist threats and other relatively short-term conditions that may pose risks to American travelers.

For more information about these documents, click the text on the travel warnings page that says What Are Consular Information Sheets, Travel Warnings & Public Announcements? (see Figure 8.2).

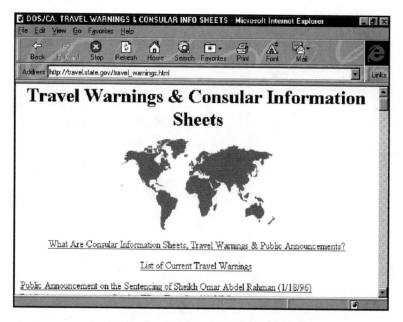

FIGURE 8.2   The Bureau of Consular Affairs' site makes it easy to monitor travel advisories.

## OTHER RESOURCES FROM THE BUREAU OF CONSULAR AFFAIRS

The Bureau of Consular Affairs offers several other useful features. To access any of the following, just click the text on their Home Page (**http://travel.state.gov**):

- **Travel Publications**—Miscellaneous information in such categories as Overseas Citizens Services, Travel Warning on Drugs Abroad, Sending Money Overseas to a U.S. Citizen in an Emergency, and Tips for Older Americans. You also can find tips for traveling to specific areas of the world.

- **International Legal Assistance**—Information for Belgium, Canada, France, Germany, Switzerland, and the United Kingdom.

- **Visit U.S. Embassy and Consulate Home Pages Worldwide**—A directory to the Web pages of embassies and consulates.

# MONITORING HEALTH ADVISORIES

The Bureau of Consulate Affairs home page also offers a link to the home page for the U.S. Centers for Disease Control and Prevention (**http://www.cdc.gov**), which provides a special section of travel information. To access it, just click the text that says Travelers' Health on the CDC's Home Page. You then will see the page pictured in part in Figure 8.3.

As you scroll down the Traveler's Health page, you'll see that you can access several different types of information:

- The Graphical Travel Map lets you point and click to find health information on a specific region.

- The Reference Material includes health information summaries, vaccine recommendations, and food and water precautions.

- The Geographic Health Recommendations offer information for specific regions and countries.

- Disease Outbreaks provides details on problem areas.

- The Additional Information section addresses miscellaneous topics such as Cholera Information, HIV/AIDS Prevention, and Japanese Encephalitis Information.

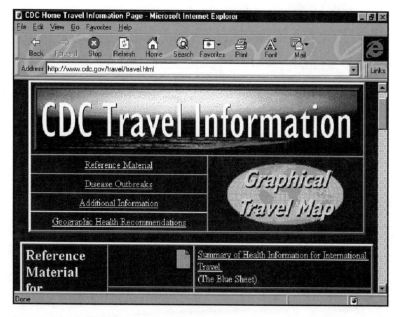

**FIGURE 8.3** The Centers for Disease Control offer health information for travelers.

## FINDING TOURISM OFFICES

If you're looking for government tourism offices and similar agencies, look in the Tourism Offices Worldwide Directory. It provides a keyword search engine that can help you find contact information for more than 1,200 official tourism organizations.

To use the directory:

1. Type the URL **http://www.mbnet.mb.ca/lucas/travel** in your Web browser's location box and press Enter.

2. The directory's home page provides the keyword search engine shown in Figure 8.4. Just type in a country name and click the Search button. Note that you also can enter specific U.S. states or Canadian provinces if you separate the country and state or province name with a slash (for example, **USA/ New York**).

3. Your search results will include an entry for the main state, province, or country office. The results also may include entries for regional offices within the area you searched. Each entry will include contact information such as the address and telephone numbers as well as the e-mail address and a link to the agency's Web site, if it has one.

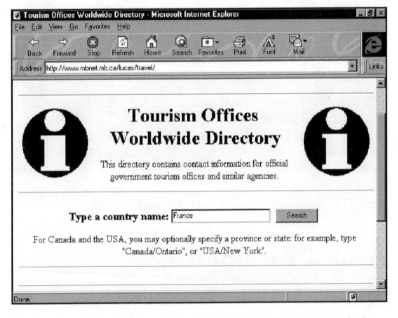

**FIGURE 8.4** The Tourism Offices Worldwide Directory can help you find contact information for more than 1,200 official tourism agencies.

In this lesson, you learned how to use government sources of travel information. In the next lesson, you'll learn how to make travel reservations online.

# Booking Travel Online

*In this lesson, you'll learn how to use the Internet to make flight, rental car, and hotel reservations.*

## Expeditions with Expedia

During the past year or so, several Web sites have begun offering online travel reservation services. One of the best is Microsoft's Expedia. After you register with the site (it's free), you can use Expedia's Travel Agent system, which is a Web version of the same system many travel agencies use.

You can use the system to find a flight, car, and room for your trip. You can make reservations online and pay for them with your credit card through a secure connection (see below). You also can create detailed itineraries, set up a fare tracking program, and take advantage of numerous other travel features at the site.

This lesson shows you how to create a complete itinerary with flight, rental car, and hotel bookings, so it involves a lot of steps. But most of them take only a second or two. Plus, after you've gone through the process once, you'll be able to do it more quickly in the future.

Please note that you will not need to make actual reservations during this lesson. So feel free to explore the system as much as you want. To get started:

1. Type the URL **http://expedia.msn.com/** in your Web browser's location box and press Enter.

2. On Expedia's Home Page, click the text that says Expedia Travel Agent (see Figure 9.1).

**Secure Connection**   This is a connection to the Internet that uses a security protocol designed to protect the privacy and authenticity of online information (credit card numbers, for example). To use a secure connection, you need a Web browser that supports it. Both Netscape Navigator and Internet Explorer do. To use their security features, you don't need to do anything other than click on a link that says you will begin using a secure connection. Your browser then will display a message that you are about to enter a secure area. When you enter the area, Internet Explorer displays the image of a lock on the browser's status bar. Netscape Navigator displays the image of a whole key instead of broken key. How secure is a secure connection? Most experts agree that it's about as safe as ordering something over the phone with a credit card. To keep up-to-date on fraud alerts, visit the site for the National Fraud Information Center (**http://www.fraud.com**). The site also offers tips for safe shopping on the Web.

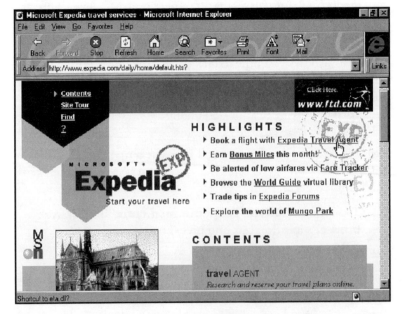

**Figure 9.1**   Expedia offers many services for travelers, including the Travel Agent online reservation system.

3. On the next page, click Registration.

4. On the Registration Options page, click the box to set up a free Expedia account and password. If you're a member of the Microsoft Network, click the box that lets you use your MSN Member ID and password. If your browser supports a secure connection, click the box under Security Register. When you've completed the page, click the Continue button at the bottom.

5. Fill in the registration page, read the Expedia Membership Agreement, and click the I ACCEPT button. Then click Back to Travel Agent.

6. On the Travel Agent main page, click the text that says Shop for Flights, Cars, and Hotels.

7. Click Start a new Itinerary.

8. Scroll down the New Itinerary page and click the Flight Wizard icon.

9. On the first Flight Wizard page, select the type of trip you're seeking. Also select the ticket class and number of passengers by clicking the appropriate boxes. For this lesson, feel free to make up the details of a hypothetical trip. Then click the Continue bar near the bottom of the page.

10. The next page lets you type the name of your departure city, airport name, or airport code in the From box. Then type your destination city or airport in the To box. (If the information you enter isn't specific enough, Travel Agent will present another page that helps you choose a particular airport.) You also should enter your departing and arriving dates and times. Enter the date in the MM/DD/YY format. Click the View Calendar bar if you want to choose a date from an online calendar. Click Continue when you finish.

11. The Search Options page lets you choose the airline and type of flights you want. Click the appropriate boxes and then click Continue.

12. Your search results will include all the flights that meet
    your criteria. To see details on a specific flight, click the
    underlined price next to the listing (see Figure 9.2). You
    then can use the Back button on your browser to return
    to the main list.

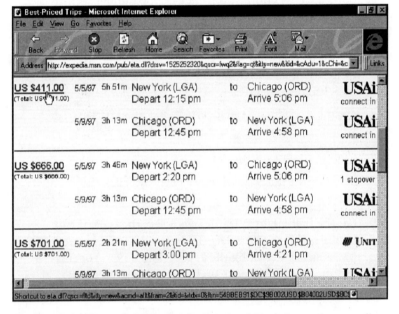

**FIGURE 9.2** Expedia's Travel Agent provides information on all
the flights meeting your criteria.

13. When you find a flight you like, scroll to the bottom of
    the flight detail page. You'll see that you can choose to
    reserve the flight, add it to your itinerary, or cancel the
    reservation process. For this lesson, click Add to Itinerary.
    Also be sure to click the box that indicates you agree with
    the rules and penalties of the fare. Remember, you're not
    making an actual reservation at this time.

14. Expedia's Travel Agent will display your flight informa-
    tion in your itinerary and let you select from several icons

on the left side of the screen. Click the one labeled Car Wizard.

15. On the Search for a Car page, you'll see that Travel Agent has used the information you entered in the Flight Wizard to fill in the boxes for the location and dates you may need the car. Of course, you can override this information if you wish. On the same page you can choose the type of car and preferred rental company. Click Continue when you're finished.

16. Your search results will include a listing of rental cars matching your criteria. You can find more details about a specific car by clicking the underlined price (see Figure 9.3).

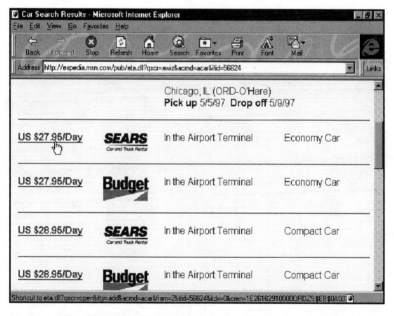

**FIGURE 9.3**  Click the underlined price to find complete details about a specific car.

17. When you view the details about a car, you can reserve it, add it to your itinerary, or cancel the car reservation process. For this lesson, click Add to Itinerary.

18. Travel Agent will display your itinerary with both the flight and rental car information. Now select the Hotel Wizard button.

19. On the Location page, you'll see that Travel Agent has used the information you entered previously to determine the city where you want to stay. You can select a specific hotel or chain. Click Continue when you're ready.

20. The next page lets you choose the prices and amenities you want. You also can choose to search only hotels that can be reserved online. If an online map is available for your city, you can select to have your search results displayed in a list or a map. For this lesson, select the list option and then click Continue.

21. Your screen will look similar to the one shown in Figure 9.4. To see details about a hotel, click its name in the list in the left frame.

**FIGURE 9.4**    Travel Agent offers detailed hotel information.

22. Click the bar labeled Check Room Availability.

23. The next page lets you specify the number of guests and the dates you'll be staying. You'll see that Travel Agent has again used the information you provided to fill in the selections. To accept them, click Continue.

24. Your search results will include a list of available rooms meeting your criteria. Click any room price for more details.

25. At the bottom of the Hotel Room Detail page, click Add to Itinerary.

26. Now you will see a complete itinerary (a sample is shown in part in Figure 9.5). You can choose to:

   - Edit, delete or print by choosing the icons on the left side of the page.

   - Make actual reservations by clicking the bars within the itinerary.

   - Travel Agent automatically saves your itinerary for you under the name of the destination and travel date.

You can open your itinerary the next time you visit the site by choosing it from the Select Itinerary page. Travel Agent will store up to six unpurchased itineraries for you.

## Expedia's Other Travel Resources

Besides Travel Agent, Expedia provides several other resources you may find helpful when you're booking business travel. Look for these features on the home page:

   - **Fare Tracker**   You can get weekly e-mail listing the best air fares between three pairs of cities you select.

   - **Forums**   Message boards that let you share travel tips with others.

- **World Guide**    An illustrated guidebook covering more than 250 destinations.

- **Travel Dispatch**    Up-to-date news for travelers.

- **Weather Watch**    Conditions and forecasts worldwide.

- **Currency Converter**    Instant information on more than 200 currencies.

# OTHER ONLINE RESERVATION SYSTEMS

The Web hosts many other notable travel sites. Here's a sampling:

- **easySABRE (http://www.easysabre.com)** is the Web version of an online reservation service that's been available through commercial online systems for more than a decade. The Web site lets you choose between the command-driven, text-based easySABRE and a point-and-click graphical version called Travelocity.

- **Biztravel.com (http://www.biztravel.com)** offers an online, reservation system as well as an interactive business travel magazine; a database of information on hotels, restaurants, weather, and airports; and a service that enables registered members to track their frequent flyer/stayer miles and points (for more information, see Lesson 17, "Using Business Travel Resources").

- **Preview Travel (http://www.reservations.com)** lets you book flights and car rentals.

- **Ticketmaster Travel (http://www.ticketmaster.com/spotl/travel/)** offers not only airline, car, and hotel reservations but also tickets for sports, theater, concert, and family events at your destination.

- **American Express (http://www.americanexpress.com)** offers airline tickets, vacation specials, and a section of Last Minute Travel Bargains.

- Many airlines are now offering their own Internet reservation systems and information about bargain fares for online users. Several airline sites will let you sign up to receive regular e-mail about discounts. To find the Web address of a specific airline, you can use the search engines explained in Lesson 5 or the directories described in Lesson 6. But first, try **Airlines on the Web (http://www.itn.net/airlines)**. It provides an extensive guide to the Web sites of commercial airlines worldwide. You also can follow links to frequent flyer programs and other airline-related sites.

- **The World Wide Wanderer (http://www.tmn. com/wwwanderer/WWWanderer_home_page. html)** may help you find a "bucket shop" that can save you up to seventy percent on flights from anywhere in the U.S., U.K., and Canada to destinations around the world. Bucket shops are discount travel agencies that broker tickets not sold to business travelers. Bucket shops are most useful for travelers who know where they want to go but are flexible about the departure and return dates.

- **Travel Discounters (http://www.traveldis-counters.com)** promises $50-$150 off airline fares above $300. The offer is valid for the forty-eight contiguous United States on travel via Continental, TWA, American, Northwest, and United. Visit Travel Discounters' site for complete details.

In this lesson, you learned how to book travel online. In the next lesson, you'll learn how to access online travel agents and tour operators.

# 10

# FINDING ONLINE TRAVEL AGENTS AND TOUR OPERATORS

*In this lesson, you'll learn how to find Web sites sponsored by travel agencies and tour companies.*

## USING A TRAVEL AGENT DATABASE

The last lesson showed you how to use the Web to be your own travel agent, but for some trips you still may want the services of travel professionals. You can use the Web to find them, too.

A resource that will help is called ASTAnet. Sponsored by the American Society of Travel Agents, the world's largest travel-trade organization, ASTAnet provides an online agency-finder and links to members with Web sites.

To use ASTAnet, follow these instructions:

1. Type the URL **http://www.astanet.com** in your Web browser's location box and press Enter.

2. On the home page, click the text that says ASTA Travel Directory (see Figure 10.1).

3. Scroll down the next page until you see the search entry boxes pictured in Figure 10.2. Note that you will not need to fill in all the boxes; you can fill in any combination to pinpoint the type of agency you're trying to find.

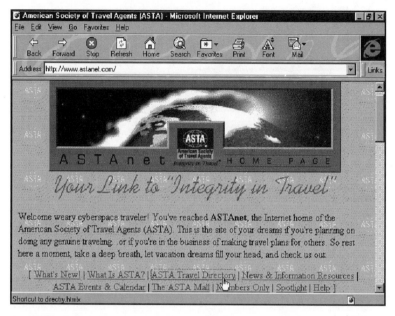

**FIGURE 10.1** The American Society of Travel Agents offers an online agency finder.

4. In the Company Type scrollbox, you can choose to look for travel agencies, tour operators, and several other different types of travel and transportation companies. You can also select All Choices.

5. If you're looking for a specific company, enter its name in the Company Name box. You can use partial names.

6. If you're looking for all travel agencies in a specific location or ZIP code, fill in either of those boxes and leave the Company Name box empty. The location can be a city, state, country, or three letter airport code (LAX for the Los Angeles International airport, for example).

7. On the other hand, you may want to leave the name, location, and ZIP code boxes empty and use the scroll boxes near the bottom of the page to select a type of specialty travel, a destination, or both.

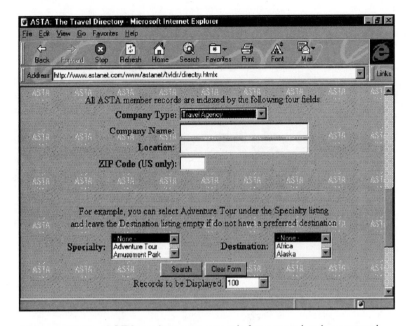

**Figure 10.2**    ASTAnet lets you search for agencies by several different criteria.

8. After you make your selections, choose a number from the Records to be Displayed scrollbox, or leave it set at 100.

9. Click the Search button.

10. Your results will include a list of the names and addresses of all the agencies matching your search criteria. If you click an agency's name, you'll receive more detailed information. For some agencies, the links will take you directly to their Web sites.

ASTAnet also offers several other features you may find useful. Look for these on the Home Page (see Figure 10.1):

- **What's New!**   News about the travel industry.

- **What Is ASTA?**   Information on the association.

- **News & Information Resources**   An electronic library of travel news and trip planning information.

- **ASTA Events & Calendar**   Details on travel industry events.

- **The ASTA Mall**   Information on ASTA-endorsed products such as the TravelPlus credit card.

# OTHER RESOURCES AND DIRECTORIES

Here are the Web sites of a few other directories and large agencies.

- The Travel Agency Directory (**http://www.tenio. com/tad/**) lists contact information for more than 31,000 agencies. You can search by keyword or ZIP code.

- AAA offers a Web site (**http://www.aaa.com**) that lists all its offices and travel agencies. You can find preferred deals for members as well as miscellaneous tips and maps for motorists.

- Carlson Wagonlit (**http://www.travel.carlson.com/**) offers a worldwide agency locator. You also can find travel tips, an online newsletter, and advice on traveling with kids.

- The Adventure Tour Directory (**http://www.csn.net/ trips/**) lets you browse through such categories as Dude/ Guest Ranch, Educational and Nature Tours, International Adventures, and Travel Agencies that work with Adventure Tour Programs. If you're interested in adventure tours, see also Lesson 19, "Exploring Adventure and Recreation Travel."

- Yahoo! offers extensive guides to online travel agencies and tour operators. Use the URL **http://www.yahoo. com,** and select the following categories: Business and Economy, Companies, Travel Options. Then select either Agents or Tour Operators.

- Many of the directories listed in Lesson 6, "Using Transportation and Travel Directories," include sections with information on agencies and tour companies. See, for example, The Travel Weekly Online section of Reed's Traveler.Net (**http://www.traveler.net/two/**).

- Travel Source (**http://www.travelsource.com/**) represents more than 40 tour operators specializing in such adventures as safaris, wine tours, cycling, villa rentals, trekking, spas, rafting, yachting, resorts, scuba diving, and much more (see Figure 10.3).

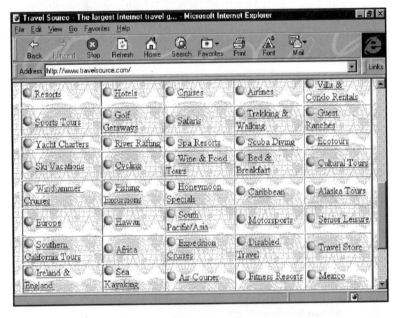

**FIGURE 10.3**    Travel Source offers information on more than 40 tour operators.

In this lesson, you learned how to find travel agencies and tour operators. In the next lesson, you'll learn how to generate online maps.

# GENERATING ONLINE MAPS

*In this lesson, you'll learn how create customized maps and find door-to-door driving instructions.*

## GOING ON A MAPQUEST

MapQuest is a service that provides maps to Web sites such as City.Net, which was described in Lesson 7, "Finding Destination Information." MapQuest also offers electronic, interactive maps and other features through its own site. To explore MapQuest's services, look for the following links on the main screen and in the left column (see Figure 11.1):

- The **Interactive Atlas** lets you create detailed maps of virtually any address in the U.S. (step-by-step instructions are listed on the next page). Maps for cities and countries around the world are available, too.

- **TripQuest** helps you find driving instructions for parts of the U.S., Canada, and Mexico (brief instructions are available near the end of this lesson).

- **Personalized Mapping** lets you create customized maps.

- **Map Shortcuts** lets you jump directly to a specific map by selecting a city or country name from a list or an interactive world map.

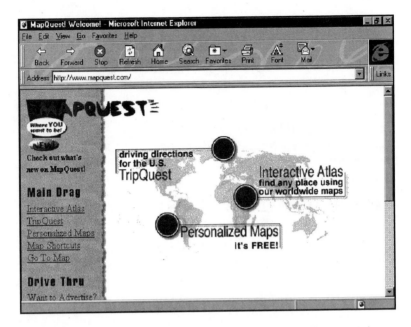

FIGURE 11.1    MapQuest offers several powerful online mapping features.

To use the MapQuest Interactive Atlas, follow these steps:

1. Type the URL **http://www.mapquest.com** in your Web browser's location box and press Enter.

2. On the MapQuest Home Page, click the Interactive Atlas icon (see Figure 11.1).

3. On the next page, you'll see the words Original, Java, and Active X beneath the Interactive Atlas logo. The terms refer to the interfaces you can use to access the atlas. When you first visit the page, you're using the Original interface. If your browser supports Java or ActiveX, you can click one of those words to see if you prefer that type of interface. For this lesson, stay with the Original interface by scrolling down the page until you see the search entry boxes shown in Figure 11.2.

**Java**  A computer language designed by Sun Microsystems. It lets users access animation, moving text, and interactive programs on a Web site.

 **ActiveX**  A Microsoft technology built into Internet Explorer 3.0 and later versions. ActiveX lets users run advanced programs such as animation on the Web. A plug-in is required to run the ActiveX Interactive Atlas with Netscape Navigator.

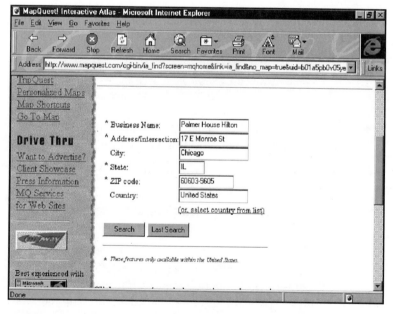

**FIGURE 11.2**  The Interactive Atlas can generate a map of virtually any U.S. business address.

4. To find a map of a U.S. address, enter as much information as possible in the search form. Don't include apartment or floor numbers. In Figure 11.2, the researcher has entered the name and address of a Chicago hotel. You also can search for a street intersection (for example, Haight St and Ashbury St). To move quickly between the fields in the search entry screen, use Tab on your keyboard.

**Can't Find an Address?**    If you can't find a business at a particular address, try entering a city and state but leaving the address blank.

**Searching by ZIP Code**    Besides searching by city name, you can search by ZIP code only. This can be a useful way to map a segment of a large city.

5. Click the Search button. The system will create your map with a star marking your location (see Figure 11.3).

6. Once you create a map, there are several things you can do with it:

   • The zoom bar on the right side of the screen lets you change the map from the national level to the street level.

   • The radio buttons directly below the map let you recenter, zoom in, and identify an icon. Click the button you want and then click the map. The Identify Icon button shows the name and address of a Point of Interest.

   • Beneath the radio buttons, the Scroll feature (not shown in Figure 11.3) lets you move the map in eight directions. Just click one of the points to shift the map in the direction you want.

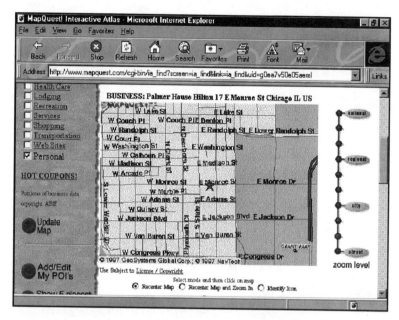

**FIGURE 11.3**   MapQuest pinpoints the location you're trying to find.

- Also beneath the radio buttons, the Customize Map Options button lets you change the look of your map. For example, you can change it from a detailed color map to a shades-of-gray map that doesn't show railroads or streams.

- MapQuest lets you display Points of Interest in such categories as Dining and Lodging. Look for the Points of Interest section on the left side of the screen (part of the section is shown in Figure 11.3). Select Points of Interest by clicking the small white check boxes next to the category names. Then click the Update Map button.

- Each Points of Interest category contains subcategories. To view them, click a category name. Your screen then will display a Points of Interest page for that category. In the Dining category, for example, you can choose such subcategories as coffee shops, fast food, various ethnic restaurants, and Internet cafes. Click the boxes next to the subcategories you want, and then click the Update Map button.

- The Add/Edit My POIs button lets you define and save your own Points of Interest for businesses, landmarks, services, and facilities.

7. When you're happy with your map, you can print or save it. To print, just click the Print button on your Web browser. To save, click the My Maps button on the MapQuest screen. You also can load and delete maps you've saved before.

# CREATING DOOR-TO-DOOR DRIVING INSTRUCTIONS

Another MapQuest feature is called TripQuest. It can generate city-to-city driving directions for the entire U.S. and parts of Canada and Mexico. It even can create door-to-door directions for addresses in major metropolitan areas.

To use this feature, follow these steps:

1. Click the text that says TripQuest either on the MapQuest Home Page (see Figure 11.1) or on the menu bar on the left side of the screen.

2. You'll see a simple interface that lets you enter your starting point and destination (see Figure 11.4). For city-to-city directions, just fill in the city and state or province boxes. For door-to-door directions, add street addresses.

3. Click either Door-to-Door or City-to-City.

4. Click the Route It! button.

5. If MapQuest doesn't have information for your starting point or destination, you'll receive a message. If MapQuest does have the information, you'll receive step-by-step driving directions, number of miles, and links to maps.

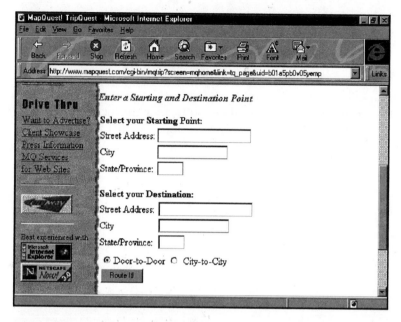

**FIGURE 11.4**    You can generate step-by-step driving instructions with TripQuest.

# USING OTHER ONLINE MAPPING RESOURCES

MapQuest offers some of the best electronic maps on the Web, but there are a few other sites you also may want to try:

- Rand McNally Online (**http://www.randmcnally. com**) provides an online database of information on road construction. Look in the site's travel tools section.

- DeLorme's CyberRouter (**http://route.delorme.com/**) lets you generate maps and driving instructions between more than 240,000 places in the U.S. The CyberRouter page also includes a link to a CyberAtlas.

- Maps On Us (**http://www.mapsonus.com/ index.cgi/**) offers mapping and routing features as well as an electronic yellow pages.

- AutoPilot (**http://www.freetrip.com/**) provides a Highway Trip Planning System that lets you create personalized itineraries. They can include the locations of hotels, restaurants, national parks, and other facilities along the way. You also can choose direct or scenic routes and plan a trip that avoids toll roads.

In this lesson, you learned how to create online maps and driving directions. In the next lesson, you'll learn how to track weather information.

# TRACKING WEATHER CONDITIONS AND FORECASTS

*In this lesson, you'll learn how to find online weather reports. You'll also find out how to track weather conditions and arrival times at U.S. airports.*

## FINDING WORLDWIDE WEATHER REPORTS

What's the weather going to be like for your trip? What type of clothes should you pack for your destination?

The Web can help you find the answers. Many sites offer highly detailed weather information. Intellicast, for example, provides forecasts, conditions, and maps for destinations around the world.

To use Intellicast, follow these simple instructions:

1. Type the URL **http://www.intellicast.com** in your Web browser's address box and press Enter.

2. On the Home Page, click the text that says USA Weather. It will give you access to the National Weather Outlook, which includes an interactive map (see Figure 12.1). Just click on a city to get a four-day forecast, sophisticated radar and satellite images, and a weather almanac.

3. Use the Back button on your browser to return to the main USA Weather page. You then can find information on more cities by clicking the state abbreviations in the Complete Cities List. Beneath the cities list, you can access national radar and satellite images.

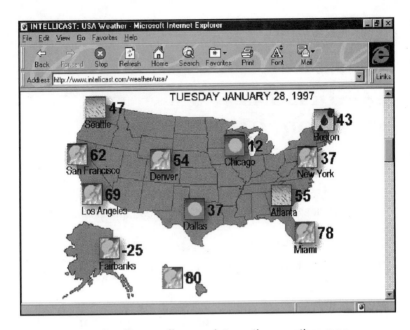

**FIGURE 12.1**    Intellicast offers an Interactive weather map.

4.  To access weather information worldwide, use the Back
    button on your browser to return to the Intellicast Home
    Page; then click World Weather.

5.  The next page will include an interactive map for World
    Weather Forecasts (see Figure 12.2). Just click an area to
    receive forecasts for that region and selected cities. Be-
    neath the weather map, you can access satellite images for
    the earth and several continents.

Intellicast also provides a Travel Cities page that offers instant
access to two-day forecasts for several U.S. cities. To access them
just click the words Travel Cities on the Intellicast Home Page. If
you then click the name of a city in the list, you'll receive the
same information you did in the USA Weather area.

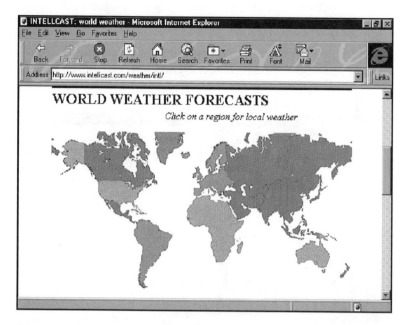

**FIGURE 12.2**    World weather forecasts also are available through an interactive map.

The Travel Cities page also offers a unique feature called the Travel Summary. If you click those words, you can receive the Intellicast Travel Forecast, an MPEG video of a television-style weather broadcast. Please note that the Travel Forecast will take several minutes to download to your computer unless you have a high-speed Internet connection.

**MPEG**    Motion Picture Experts Group is a compression standard used to make videos available through the Internet. To play the video, you need an MPEG player installed on your computer. If you don't have one, you can get it from Web sites such as Netscape Navigator Components (**http://home.netscape.com/comprod/mirror/navcomponents_download.html**), and the Microsoft Internet Explorer Download Area (**http://www.microsoft.com/ie/download/**).

# TUNING IN THE WEATHER CHANNEL

Cable television's Weather Channel offers a Web site with state-by-state and international conditions and forecasts as well as weather-related news, maps, and radar and satellite images.

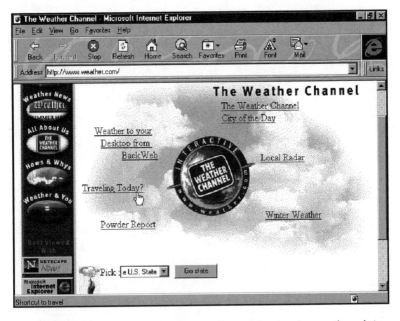

FIGURE 12.3   The Weather Channel provides basic weather data and several innovative features.

The Weather Channel also offers a unique feature for air travelers: the U.S. Travel Map, which presents an overview of airport arrival conditions across the country.

The Weather Channel updates the map every 30 minutes with average arrival conditions and every hour with weather conditions. You also can use this feature to find the arrival time for a specific flight.

To get started, follow these numbered steps:

1. Type the URL **http://www.weather.com** in your Web browser's address box and press Enter.

2. On the Weather Channel's Home Page, click the text that says Traveling Today? (see Figure 12.3). Note that the text might say Business Travelers Forecast instead.

3. You'll see a map showing the average airport arrival delay at 35 of the busiest U.S. airports (see Figure 12.4). The delays are superimposed over a weather map indicating rain, fog, and snow conditions. Note that the color of a dot on the map indicates the average amount of the delay the airport is experiencing.

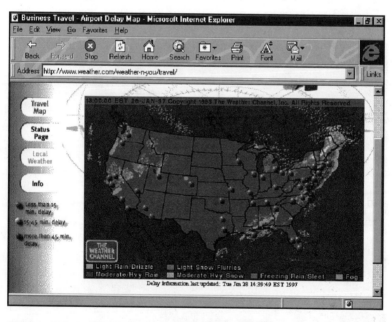

**FIGURE 12.4** The U.S. Travel Map shows weather conditions and delay times for airports across the U.S.

4. If the airport in which you're interested isn't indicated on the map, you can find information on it by clicking the tab in the left margin that says Status Page.

5. On the Status Page, select an airport from the Destination scrollbox and click the Get Delay and Set Itinerary button (see Figure 12.5). You'll receive the average arrival delay for that airport.

6. You also can use the Status Page to check the arrival time for a specific flight. Just select Departure and Destination Airports from the pulldown menu boxes. Then select the airline and type the flight number in the Airline Flight Number box. When you click the Get Delay button, you'll receive the estimated arrival time for your flight as well as the average delay for your destination airport.

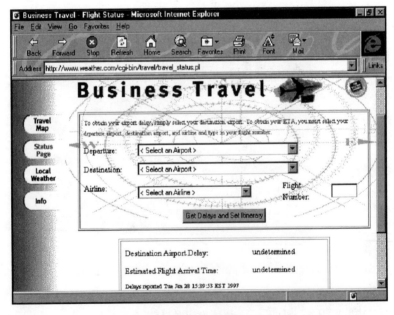

**FIGURE 12.5** The Status Page lets you check not only airport delays but also specific flight arrival times.

7. If you click the Local Weather tab in the left margin you can receive five-day forecasts and current conditions for your departure and destination cities. Besides the 100 airport cities, you also can use the Local Weather page to check the weather conditions for about 1,200 other U.S. cities. Just select the appropriate state from the Quickfinder scrollbox.

If you use Windows 95, the Weather Channel can also deliver information automatically to your desktop. For complete details on this service, click the MyWay button on the Weather Channel's Home Page.

# OTHER WEATHER RESOURCES

Here are a few other sites you may want to check before your trip:

- AccuWeather (**http://www.accuweather.com**) offers a free service that includes real-time updates of local forecasts, NEXRAD Doppler Radar, ten-day outlooks, satellite images, and maps.

- Current Weather Maps/Movies (**http://clunix.cl. msu.edu/weather/**), from Michigan State University, offers sophisticated weather images (the latest pass of a weather satellite, for example).

- The Travelocity online reservation system (**http:// www.travelocity.com**) offers travel forecasts and airport reports for North America, Asia, and Europe. Click the word Weather in the menu bar in the site's Destinations & Interests section.

- Landings, a Web site for pilots and aviation enthusiasts, offers a section that promises "every weather link known" (**http://www.landings.com/_landings/pages/ weather.html**).

In this lesson, you learned how to find online weather information. In the next lesson, you'll learn how to use a currency converter.

# 13

# USING A CURRENCY CONVERTER

*In this lesson, you'll learn how to find foreign exchange information.*

## ACCESSING OLSEN & ASSOCIATES TECHNOLOGY

So you're going to Norway and you want to know how many kroners you can get for your dollars? You can find out the exchange rate for kroners and 163 other currencies at a site created by Olsen & Associates, a developer of online forecasting technology for business and finance.

Data provided through the O&A converter is comparable to the exchange rates published in *The Wall Street Journal*. O&A provides averages for the global foreign exchange market gathered from several sources, including Telerate, Knight Ridder, and Reuters.

O&A updates the information daily at 06:00 MET (Middle European Time) with information from the previous day. Using the converter is very easy:

1. Type the URL **http://www.olsen.ch/cgi-bin/ exmenu** in your Web browser's location box and press Enter.

2. In the left scrollbox, click the name of the currency you want to convert from (see Figure 13.1).

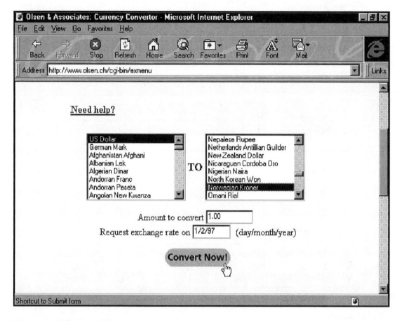

**FIGURE 13.1**    Olsen & Associates can help you find exchange rates for 164 currencies.

3.  In the right scrollbox, click the name of the currency you want to convert to.

4.  Type the sum you want to convert in the Amount to convert box.

5.  If you want to find the exchange rate for a date other than yesterday (the default), type a new date in the appropriate box. For most currencies, you can view an exchange rate for any day since January 1, 1990 (remember: the data is always one day old).

6.  Click the Convert Now! button.

7.  You will receive the exchange rate and details on recent foreign exchange market activity (see Figure 13.2).

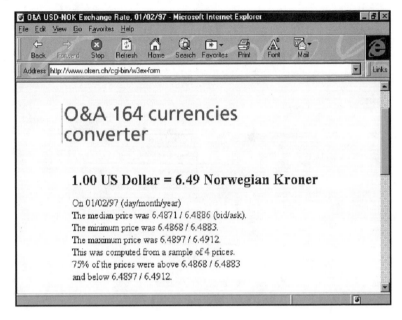

**FIGURE 13.2**   The O&A converter provides the exchange rate and details on how it was computed.

**Why does the bank offer different rates?**   Your bank may advertise slightly different exchange rates than those you find through the Olsen & Associates converter. Why? Here's how O&A explains it: "The prices quoted on the O&A currency converter are based on interbank market rates and generally reflect the exchange rates for transactions of US $1 million or more. Retail spreads (the difference between the buy and sell prices) for smaller amounts are not reflected in these prices since they vary from country to country and often from bank to bank."

# USING XENON LABORATORIES' UNIVERSAL CURRENCY CONVERTER

The Canadian technology company Xenon Laboratories has created The Universal Currency Converter (**http://www.xe.net/ currency**). It's a simple program (see Figure 13.3), similar to the one provided by Olsen & Associates.

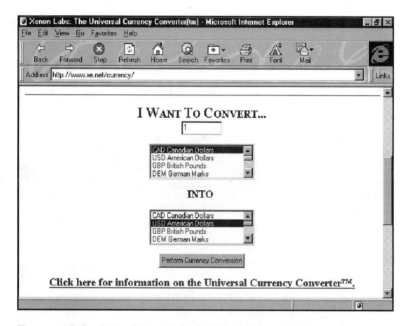

**FIGURE 13.3**   Like Olsen & Associates, Xenon Laboratories offers an easy-to-use currency converter.

The currency converter page is available not only in English but also in Spanish and Swedish. To change the page to one of those languages, just click the appropriate text near the top of the page (not shown in Figure 13.3).

Xenon also provides an Interactive Currency Table that lets you generate a list of exchange rates across several currencies. To use the Interactive Currency Table, follow these steps.

1. Type the URL **http://www.xe.net/currency** in your Web browser's location box and press Enter.

2. Near the top of the home page, click the text Interactive Currency Table.

3. Select a base currency in the scrollbox under the heading SHOW ME A CURRENCY TABLE IN UNITS OF....

4. Click the Generate Currency Table button.

5. You will receive a table similar to that shown in part in Figure 13.4.

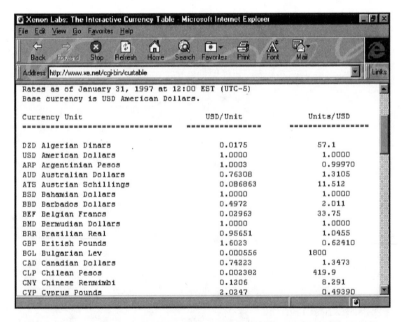

Rates as of January 31, 1997 at 12:00 EST (UTC-5)
Base currency is USD American Dollars.

| Currency Unit | USD/Unit | Units/USD |
|---|---|---|
| DZD Algerian Dinars | 0.0175 | 57.1 |
| USD American Dollars | 1.0000 | 1.0000 |
| ARP Argentinian Pesos | 1.0003 | 0.99970 |
| AUD Australian Dollars | 0.76308 | 1.3105 |
| ATS Austrian Schillings | 0.086863 | 11.512 |
| BSD Bahamian Dollars | 1.0000 | 1.0000 |
| BBD Barbados Dollars | 0.4972 | 2.011 |
| BEF Belgian Francs | 0.02963 | 33.75 |
| BMD Bermudian Dollars | 1.0000 | 1.0000 |
| BRR Brazilian Real | 0.95651 | 1.0455 |
| GBP British Pounds | 1.6023 | 0.62410 |
| BGL Bulgarian Lev | 0.000556 | 1800 |
| CAD Canadian Dollars | 0.74223 | 1.3473 |
| CLP Chilean Pesos | 0.002382 | 419.9 |
| CNY Chinese Renmimbi | 0.1206 | 8.291 |
| CYP Cyprus Pounds | 2.0247 | 0.49390 |

**FIGURE 13.4** The American dollar was chosen as the base unit for this Interactive Currency Table.

Xenon also offers a free Currency Update Service that lets you receive currency table updates automatically by electronic mail. An update is sent every business day, except holidays. For more information, see the site's subscription page (**http://www. xe.net/currency/subscrib.htm**).

At this writing, Xenon is negotiating with several financial data firms for a real-time currency rate feed. It should greatly expand the site's list of supported currencies.

# OTHER ONLINE CURRENCY CONVERTERS

Here are a few more online currency converters that you can access:

- The Travelocity online reservation service (**http:// www.travelocity.com**) offers a version of The Universal Currency Converter. Look in the Destinations & Interests section and click the word Currency in the menu bar near the top of the page.

- *The Washington Post* offers U.S. dollar rates for about 100 currencies (**http://www.washingtonpost.com/wp-srv/business/longterm/stocks/currency.htm**). Rates are updated at 5 a.m., noon, and 7 p.m. EDT every day currencies are traded.

- Microsoft's Expedia (**http://www.expedia.com**) offers a converter with a list of most common currencies. You can click a button to expand the list to include more than 200 currencies. That's more than the other sites noted in this lesson, but the rate information in Expedia isn't updated every day. After you perform a conversion, check the date on the left side of the screen to find out when the last update occurred.

In this lesson, you learned how to use currency converters. In the next lesson, you'll learn how to find foreign language information.

# 14

## LESSON

# FINDING FOREIGN LANGUAGE INFORMATION

*In this lesson, you'll learn how to find and use foreign language resources for travelers.*

## ACCESSING ONLINE AUDIO AT FODOR'S

Fodor's Web site is mentioned in several other lessons in this book because it provides many valuable resources for travelers. One of them is a section containing foreign language information.

The information has been published on the Web with the help of Living Language, one of the leading names in foreign language instruction. The company's courses, originally developed by government experts for overseas-bound diplomats, are available on books, cassettes, CDs, and CD-ROMs in 15 different languages.

Fodor's site offers information on four languages: French, German, Italian, and Spanish. The site lets you read and hear phrases categorized by topics such as At the Airport, Dining Out, Health Care, and Shopping.

To use Fodor's foreign language feature, follow these steps:

1. Type the URL **http://www.fodors.com** in your Web browser's location box and press Enter.

2. On Fodor's Home Page, click Know Before You Go.

3. On the next page, click the text Language for Travelers.

4. Now you can select a language and topic (see Figure 14.1). Click the radio button to either French, German, Italian, or Spanish.

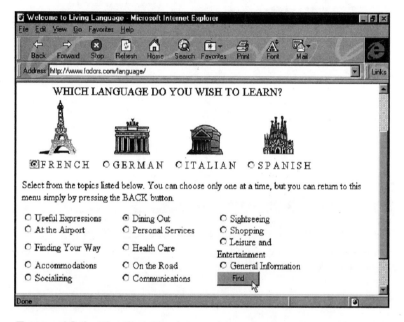

**FIGURE 14.1** The Fodor's site provides phrases on specific topics in four languages.

5. Click the radio button next to one of the topics. In Figure 14.1 the traveler has selected Dining Out. Note that you can choose only one topic at a time.

6. Click the Find button.

7. The next page will display phrases in English, in the language you selected, and in phonetic spelling (see Figure 14.2). To hear a phrase spoken aloud, click the highlighted text in the foreign language.

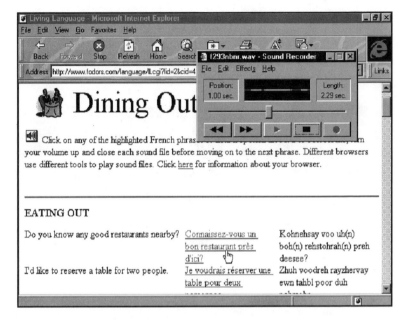

**FIGURE 14.2**    With most Web browsers, you can hear the phrases spoken aloud simply by clicking them. This figure shows a WAV audio player, which appears when you're listening to the files.

**Help with Sound Files**    The sound files you hear through the Fodor's site are WAV files. WAV is an audio format (pronounced "wave") that recent versions of most Web browsers will play easily. All you need to do is point, click, and listen. To play the files through some older browsers, you may need to install a helper application on your computer. If you have any problems, click the word "here" in the sentence "Click here for more information about your browser" on the Fodor's page (see Figure 14.2).

**For Best Results** When you're listening to the audio files, Fodor's suggests you turn the volume up on your computer and close the player for each sound file before you pick another.

# ACCESSING FOREIGN LANGUAGE INFORMATION AT TRAVLANG

Travlang is a Web sitethat offers information on more than 40 languages. To use Travlang, follow these steps:

1. Type the URL **http://www.travlang.com** in your Web browser's location box and press Enter.

2. Click Languages for Travelers near the top of Travlang's Home Page. Travlang offers access to many other resources on its Home Page. You can find links to numerous translating dictionaries as well as a guide to general travel resources on the Web.

3. The next page lets you select a native language in the scrollbox (see Figure 14.3).

4. Select the language you want to learn by clicking the appropriate flag or text.

5. The next page lets you choose the category of words and phrases you want to study. You can choose from Basic Words, Numbers, Shopping/Dining, Travel, Directions, Places, and Time and Dates. Just click the radio button beside the category you're interested in.

6. Click the Submit button.

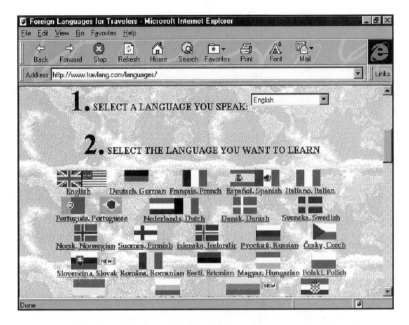

FIGURE 14.3    Travlang provides information for more than 40 languages.

7. You will see a list of words and phrases in your native language as well as translations in the language you selected (see Figure 14.4).

8. To listen to a word or phrase, click the translation. The files are in the AU audio format, which, like the WAV format mentioned previously, should play through the latest versions of most Web browsers. If you have any problems, click Sound Help Page. To avoid computer memory problems, close the player after you listen to each file.

9. If you click the Take a quick quiz! button at the top of the page, you can take a multiple-choice test of your knowledge of a language.

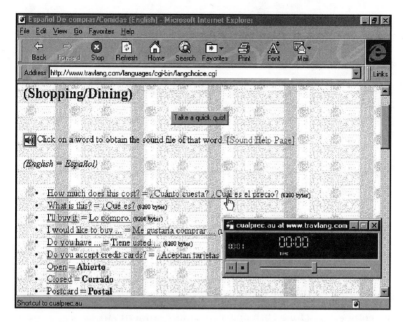

**FIGURE 14.4** Travlang offers audio files in the AU format. This figure shows an AU player.

As mentioned previously, Travlang's Home Page offers links to several online dictionaries. Just click the words Translating Dictionaries on the site's Home Page and you'll have access to dictionaries for German, Dutch, French, Spanish, Danish, Portuguese, and Afrikaans.

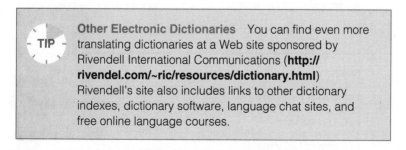

**Other Electronic Dictionaries**   You can find even more translating dictionaries at a Web site sponsored by Rivendell International Communications (**http://rivendel.com/~ric/resources/dictionary.html**) Rivendell's site also includes links to other dictionary indexes, dictionary software, language chat sites, and free online language courses.

In this lesson, you learned how to find foreign language information. In the next lesson, you'll learn how to use travel newsgroups.

# 15 PARTICIPATING IN TRAVEL NEWSGROUPS

*In this lesson, you'll learn how to participate in Internet newsgroups. You'll also learn how to gather information from them using a search engine on the Web.*

## WHAT ARE NEWSGROUPS?

The term newsgroup is something of a misnomer. Newsgroups actually are electronic message boards that let you read comments from others and post your own.

Developed by Duke University graduate students in 1979, newsgroups are primarily text-based forums that predate the Web. They often are called Usenet (User's Network) groups because Usenet is the system that hosts most newsgroups.

There's a newsgroup for virtually any topic you can think of, including several newsgroups where you can find discussions of travel and related topics. Here's a sampling:

- **alt.vacation.las-vegas**
- **misc.kids.vacation**
- **rec.arts.disney.parks**
- **rec.outdoor.national-parks**
- **rec.parks.theme**
- **rec.travel.air**
- **rec.travel.africa**
- **rec.travel.asia**
- **rec.travel.caribbean**
- **rec.travel.cruises**
- **rec.travel.europe**
- **rec.travel.latin-america**
- **rec.travel.marketplace**
- **rec.travel.misc**
- **rec.travel.usa-canada**

**Moderated Newsgroups** If you visit newsgroups often, you probably will come across a group that says it's moderated. That means the group is monitored by its organizers to help eliminate off-topic messages, scam artists (see below), and flames (insults to other newsgroup users).

**Avoiding Scams** You should treat all information you find on the Internet with caution. This is especially true of the solicitations you find in newsgroups. The groups are notorious hosts of advertising for get-rich-quick schemes and phony offers for merchandise or services. To protect yourself, never give out credit card, bank account, or telephone numbers in a newsgroup.

You need a browser to access the Web; similarly, you need a newsreader to access newsgroups. Later versions of Internet Explorer and Netscape Navigator include built-in newsreading software. Netscape Communicator, the "Open Email, Groupware, and Browser Suite," includes a program called Collabra, which provides newsgroup access because it incorporates the Network News Transfer Protocol (NNTP), an open Internet standard for newsgroup discussions.

If you use an Internet Service Provider, you probably received a newsreader with the other software the ISP provided. Contact the ISP if you need help setting up the program. Information on another powerful program you can use is available later in this lesson under the heading "Downloading a Newsreader from the Internet." If you use an online service such as America Online, you can use the service's built-in newsreading software.

# PARTICIPATING IN NEWSGROUPS VIA AMERICA ONLINE

To use AOL's built-in newsgroup program, follow these simple steps:

1. Click Internet Connection on the Channels display, and then click the Newsgroups icon. Or click the Keyword button on the main screen, type **Usenet** or **Newsgroups**, and click the Go button.

2. Before you start exploring groups, you may want to read the files listed in the scrollbox at the left of the newsgroup window (see Figure 15.1). These files contain basic information about using newsgroups. To read one, double-click the file name.

3. To browse newsgroups, click the Read My Newsgroups button. A window will open that shows the newsgroups AOL already has subscribed you to. They cover computer topics and a few general-interest subjects.

4. To open a newsgroup, double-click its name in the window.

5. You'll see a list of messages. Scan it to find a topic of interest. When you do, double-click the name of the message. The content will be displayed in a window (see Figure 15.2).

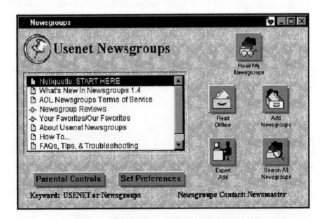

**FIGURE 15.1** America Online offers a built-in newsreading program.

The buttons on AOL's newsreader can help you navigate and reply to newsgroup messages:

- **Previous**   Takes you to the message before the one you're viewing.

- **More**   Displays more of a long message.

- **Next**   Takes you to the message after the one you're viewing.

- **Mark Unread**   After you read a message, AOL won't display it again. If you think you may want to read it again, click Mark Unread so it won't be hidden.

- **Reply to Group**   Lets you post a response to a newsgroup message.

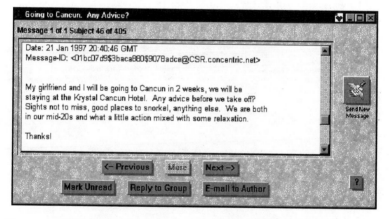

**FIGURE 15.2**   This message, taken from a travel newsgroup, shows how people use the groups to seek advice.

- **E-mail to Author**   Lets you send e-mail to the author of a message. Your e-mail will not become part of the newsgroup.

- **?**   Opens the AOL help files.

- **Send New Message**   Lets you start a new topic in a newsgroup.

## ADDING NEWSGROUPS IN AOL

AOL initially subscribes you to about a dozen groups. Subscribing to others is easy:

1. Click the Expert Add button on the main Usenet Newsgroups window (see Figure 15.1).

2. In the box that appears (Figure 15.3), type the name of a newsgroup. You can use any of the travel newsgroups' names listed in the first part of this lesson.

3. Click the Add button. The newsgroup will appear in your list the next time you open Read My Newsgroups.

Another way to subscribe to newsgroups in AOL is by using the Add Newsgroups button on the Usenet Newsgroups window (Figure 15.1). It lets you browse categories of newsgroups, topics, and messages. If you find a group you like, just click the Add button.

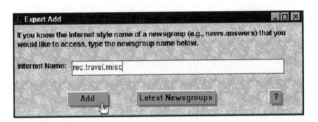

**FIGURE 15.3** AOL offers an easy way to subscribe to newsgroups.

**Finding Newsgroups' Names** To find the names of newsgroups you may be interested in, click the Search All Newsgroups button on AOL's main Usenet Newsgroups window (Figure 15.1). You can use a simple keyword search engine to find groups on particular topics. For example, you'll be able to find several groups simply by searching with the keyword **travel**.

# DOWNLOADING A NEWSREADER FROM THE INTERNET

If you access the Internet through an ISP, you can download and use sophisticated newsreading programs. For example, Forte, Inc. (**http://www.forteinc.com**) offers a freeware version of its Agent newsreader for Windows. To get a copy:

1. Type the URL **http://www.forteinc.com/getfa/ download.htm** in your Web browser's address window and press Enter.

2. Click a download site for your geographic location from either the Windows 95/NT or the Windows 3.1 table.

3. Your Web browser may open a window asking if you want to save the file or open it with a helper application. Select Save.

4. When the download is complete, scroll to the top of the Free Agent download page and click the text Free Agent Installation. You'll receive detailed instructions for installing the software.

After you've installed it, you'll be able to use several powerful newsreading features, including:

- **Browsing**   You can quickly sample newsgroups before you subscribe to them.

- **Online/offline operation**   In offline mode, Free Agent briefly connects to the Internet to get article headers. You can browse the headers offline and mark the ones that look interesting. Then Free Agent will go online again to quickly retrieve the marked articles.

- **Multitasking**   The software lets you perform several online tasks at once. For example, you can download long articles while you continue to browse a newsgroup.

- **Configurable multi-pane windows**   Free Agent, like most newsreaders, includes a window that displays a list of groups. Clicking a group name will show a list of posted messages in another window. Clicking a message will display its content in a third window. Free Agent lets you resize and rearrange the window layout.

- **Images and binary attachments**   You can post and receive messages with binary attachments. If the attachment is an image, you can view it in the newsreader.

Besides Free Agent, several other newsreaders are available through the Internet. For example, Trumpet Newsreader for Windows is a favorite among newsgroup veterans. Download a copy from **http://www.trumpet.com**. Newswatcher is a popular freeware newsreader for Macintosh. You can find it at **http://www.continuum.net/continuum/downloads/mac/news.html**.

**Know Your News Server**   Most newsreaders that are not part of an online service such as AOL require that you enter the name of your Internet Service Provider's news server in the newsreader's configuration menu. Contact your ISP if you need help.

## SEARCHING NEWSGROUP CONTENT

Several of the Web search engines discussed in Lesson 5, "Searching the Web" (for example, Excite, AltaVista, HotBot, Infoseek) let you search newsgroups in addition to Web pages. Because newsgroup search engines archive postings from the groups they cover, you can even find messages that have been deleted from the groups.

A search engine designed specifically for newsgroup content is called Deja News. It can help you find information in more than 15,000 groups.

Deja News offers both a Quick Search and a Power Search. Quick Search lets you use keywords to find matches in newsgroup postings made during the past several weeks. To use Quick Search, just type your keywords in the first window on the Deja News Home Page (see Figure 15.4).

Power Search helps you find older newsgroup messages. It also lets you use more sophisticated search strategies. To perform a Power Search:

1. Type the URL **http://www.dejanews.com/** in your Web browser's address box and press Enter.

2. Click the Power Search icon on the Deja News Home Page (see Figure 15.4).

3. On the Power Search page, type your keywords in the search entry window. Deja News supports the Boolean, proximity, and wildcard searching discussed in Lesson 5. To see how Deja News processes advanced search techniques, click the highlighted text Search For beside the search entry box

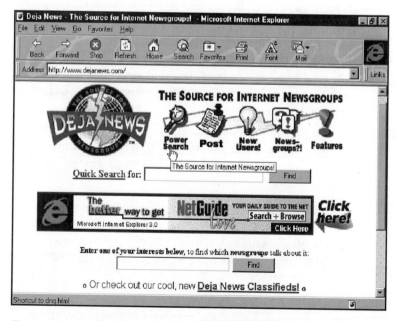

**Figure 15.4**   Deja News is a Web search engine that helps you find information in newsgroups.

4. Click the text on the Power Search page that says CREATE A QUERY FILTER. You'll see a form that will help you create a subset of newsgroup messages likely to contain the type of information you're seeking. You create the subset by limiting Deja News' entire newsgroup database to just the messages in specific newsgroups, those posted on specific dates, those from specific authors, or those focusing on specific subjects. If you need help, click the text that says Show expanded Query Filter form with examples. Or click any of the words beside the search entry windows.

5. After you've made your selections on the query filter page, click the Create Filter button.

6. Deja News will take you back to the Power Search page, but it now will include the selections you made in the Query Filter.

7. Scroll down the page to the Search Options section. It lets you customize your search and the results you'll receive according to a number of criteria, including whether you want the search engine to find all or any of your keywords, whether you want detailed or concise search results, and how you want the results sorted. Again, if you need help, click any of the highlighted words next to the search entry windows.

8. After you make your selections, scroll back to the top of the page and click the Find button. Your search results will include a list of the messages matching your search criteria.

9. To read a message, click its name. Depending on the Search Option selections you made, your results also may include such details as the date each message was posted, the newsgroup where it was posted, and the e-mail address of the author.

10. If you click the author's address, you'll see an Author Profile. It shows a statistical summary of how many times the author has posted to various newsgroups.

Deja News also includes a search engine that can help you find the names of newsgroups focusing on topics of interest. Just enter your keywords in the second search entry window on the main page (see Figure 15.4). If you want to learn more about newsgroups in general, click the Newsgroups?! icon at the top of the page.

In this lesson, you learned how to participate in Internet newsgroups. In the next lesson, you'll learn how to use electronic travel publications.

# LESSON 16

# READING ELECTRONIC TRAVEL PUBLICATIONS

*In this lesson, you'll learn how to use online travel magazines.*

## BROWSING EPICURIOUS TRAVEL

Travel writing has a long history. Occasionally, it even has had a significant impact on the world it describes. For example, Marco Polo's thirteenth-century accounts of his travels in the Far East made many other adventurers eager to find sea routes to China, Japan, and the East Indies. Nearly 200 years later, even Christopher Columbus consulted Marco Polo's writings.

In Marco Polo's time, books were copied by hand. Today, many travel writers are publishing their articles not only in printed books and magazines but also in electronic editions on the Web.

For example, Epicurious Travel (**http://travel.epicurious. com**) is the online home of the award-winning Conde Nast Traveler magazine. The site also offers directories, forums, and a great deal of travel planning information.

Here's a quick guide to the Epicurious site:

- **Places** offers information on romantic getaways, healthy trips, restaurants, cities, and more than 1,700 bed & breakfast inns.

- **Planning** includes a traveler's checklist, a deal of the week, and a weekly list of the best airfare bargains on twenty-seven of the world's most popular routes.

- **Play** includes online forums, reviews of travel books, electronic maps, and links to other Web sites.

FIGURE 16.1   Epicurious Travel combines travel writing with directories and other online resources.

- **Conde Nast Traveler Magazine** includes a destination finder, consumer help, editor's picks, a photo gallery, highlights from the print version, and an issue index.

**Epicurious for AOL Users**   According to Epicurious, the America Online Web browser doesn't display the correct images on the site's Home Page. If you're an AOL user, Epicurious suggests you use the text-only Home Page instead.

# MULTIMEDIA INFORMATION AT GLOBAL PASSAGE

Global Passage (**http://www.globalpassage.com**) is a travel e-zine (electronic magazine) published by an Australian company that specializes in Web site design (see Figure 16.2).

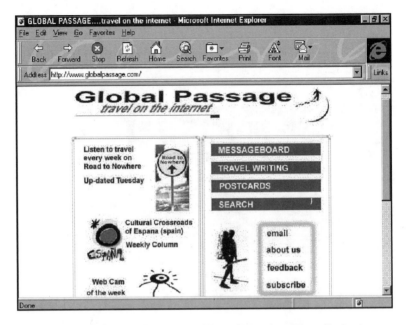

**Figure 16.2**　Global Passage offers several multimedia features.

Here's a brief guide to Global Passage:

- **Road to Nowhere** offers travel stories in the RealAudio format, an online sound format that requires a copy of the RealAudio Player installed on your computer. You can download one through a link in the Road to Nowhere area or by visiting the RealAudio site at **http://www. realaudio.com**.

- **Cultural Crossroads** is a column on the sights and sounds of Spain written by American student Amy Schmitz.

- **Weekly Web Cam** offers a live image from somewhere in the world. Archived images are available, too.

- **Messageboard** is an electronic bulletin board for posting travel notes.

- **Travel Writing** includes tales of adventures around the world.

- **Postcards** are electronic images you can send by e-mail. You even can add a message.

- **Search** offers directories of companies in the travel industry and other travel sites on the Web.

# READING NATIONAL GEOGRAPHIC ONLINE

The venerable National Geographic Society has developed a Web site that offers access to electronic editions of several publications, including *National Geographic*, *TRAVELER*, and *WORLD* magazines.

When you visit the site (**http://www.nationalgeographic. com/**), you can find excerpts from the print magazines, features prepared exclusively for cyberspace, and digital versions of the society's famous photography. For an overview of the site's numerous features, click the Help icon on the Home Page (see Figure 16.3).

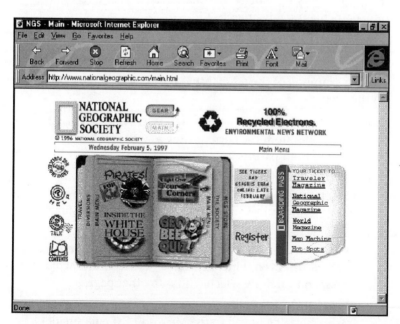

**FIGURE 16.3**  The National Geographic Society provides online versions of its popular publications.

# ARTHUR FROMMER'S OUTSPOKEN ENCYCLOPEDIA OF TRAVEL

Arthur Frommer's Outspoken Encyclopedia of Travel (**http://www.mcp.com/frommers/**) is, according to the site, "a totally comprehensive treatment of several thousands of pages on every major topic, problem, and opportunity in travel."

Outspoken opinions in the electronic encyclopedia include "forthright views on travel issues; candid advice about alternative travel, non-standard vacations, and off-beat trips; new travel approaches for thoughtful vacationers; and 'hot spots' and 'best buys' among destinations." Hundreds of pages are devoted to discounted air fares, cruises, car rentals, and accomodations.

The site promises information on savings from twenty to fifty percent. It also offers "Vacations for Real People," a daily newsmagazine focusing on budget travel. Several electronic message boards let you communicate with other travelers about sharing trips, hospitality exchanges, destination advice, and recommending particular establishments.

# OTHER ONLINE TRAVEL MAGAZINES

Here's a sampling of the many other travel publications available on the Web:

- TravelTips magazine (**http://www.trvltips.com**) offers articles from the current issue as well as a library of features from past issues.

- The Rough Guide (**http://www.hotwired.com/rough/**), part of Wired magazine's HotWired network, offers online guides to the U.S., Europe, Canada, Mexico, Australia, and Hong Kong.

- The Connected Traveler (**http://www.travelmedia.com/connected/**) includes travel stories, multimedia pages, and carefully selected links to other pages.

- Mungo Park (**http://www.mungopark.msn.com/**), a travel magazine linked to the Microsoft Expedia site described in Lesson 9, "Booking Travel Online," offers interactive, multimedia expeditions around the world.

- Web Travel Review (**http://www-swiss.ai.mit.edu/ webtravel/index.html**) offers more than 600 pages of text and 2000 photographs.

You can find a guide to many more online travel publications at Yahoo! (**http://www.yahoo.com**). Starting on the site's Home Page, select the following categories: Recreation, Travel, News and Media, Magazines.

# ONLINE BOOKSTORES FOR THE TRAVELER

You can browse virtual shelves for real ink-on-paper books at the following sites:

- The Literate Traveler (**http://www.literatetraveller. com/**) offers guidebooks and travel literature "carefully selected to enrich the travel experience and to appeal to history and literature buffs, museum-goers, art and architecture aficionados, adventurers and lovers of the good life."

- Lonely Planet (**http://www.lonelyplanet.com**) offers about 150 travel guides.

- Moon Travel Handbooks (**http://www.moon.com/**) is a publisher of guides to North America, Mexico, Central America, the Caribbean, Asia, and the Pacific Islands.

- The Adventurous Traveler Bookstore (**http://www. adventuroustraveler.com/**) offers more than 3,000 adventure books and maps.

- Amazon.com (**http://www.amazon.com**) doesn't just focus on travel titles. It's listed here because it's one of the best general bookstores on the Web. It offers a searchable database of more than a million titles in all genres.

Yahoo! also offers a directory of online travel bookstores. Select the following categories: Business and Economy, Companies, Travel, Publications, Books.

In this lesson, you learned how to access publications for travelers. In the next lesson, you'll learn how to use business travel resources.

# LESSON 17

# USING BUSINESS TRAVEL RESOURCES

*In this lesson, you'll learn how to use Web sites designed especially for business people.*

## ACCESSING BIZTRAVEL.COM

Biztravel.com (**http://www.biztravel.com**) is a Web site founded by travel industry veterans. Features available through the site's home page (see Figure 17.1) include:

- **bizTravelers** is "the travelzine for the business scene." It offers articles, news, and reviews. Travel alerts and news are updated twice a day; the full magazine is published twice a month.

- **bizCityInfo** provides information on hotels, restaurants, weather, airport information, business directories, maps, and driving directions.

- The **check-a-flight-in-progress** feature uses Flyte Trax technology to provide real-time aircraft information. You can display the exact location of a commercial plane and access an ETA based on its position and speed.

- **bizMiles** is a service that lets registered members track their miles and points in a growing roster of frequent flyer/stayer programs.

To use the bizMiles program:

1. Type the URL **http://www.biztravel.com** in your Web browser's location box and press Enter.

2. On biztravel.com's home page, click bizMiles either in the left column or on the main screen (see Figure 17.1).

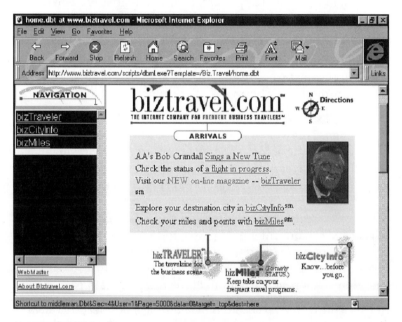

**FIGURE 17.1**   biztravel.com provides information and services for traveling professionals.

3. On the bizMiles page, click Register Now. If your browser supports a secure connection, you may want to register by clicking secure server instead. For more information about security on the Web, see the note near the beginning of Lesson 9, "Booking Travel Online".

4. Fill out the registration page. Use the Tab button on your keyboard to move between the boxes. Near the bottom of the page, you'll need to make up a Member ID and Password. As the page notes, the fields are case sensitive, which means that whenever you log on in the future, you'll need to enter your ID and Password the same way (all lowercase, all uppercase, or any combination) you did when you registered. As an easy way to remember your ID, Biztravel suggests you use your email address. After you complete the page, click Join bizMiles.

5. On the next page, read the terms and conditions and click the I Agree button.

6. You'll see the Personal Programs page. Click Add Programs. This will take you to an area where you can register using the account and PIN numbers of your frequent flyer or stayer programs. When you've finished filling out the form, Click the Register/Add Programs button.

After you've registered, any time you visit biztravel.com, you can select bizMiles and enter your password to see summaries of your accounts. For more information or if you have any problems during the registration process, click the FAQ (Frequently Asked Questions) link near the bottom of the bizMiles main page.

At this writing, biztravel.com is beta testing a new feature called bizReservations. It's a travel reservations service that, when completed, will let you book airline tickets, hotel rooms, and car rentals online.

## SEARCHING TRADE SHOW CENTRAL

If you're a business traveler looking for information on trade shows, conventions, or conferences, look no further than Trade Show Central. It's a Web site with a directory of information on more than 30,000 shows worldwide.

**FIGURE 17.2** Trade Show Central provides a directory with information on more than 30,000 shows.

To search Trade Show Central's database, follow these steps:

1. Type the URL **http://www.tscentral.com/** in your Web browser's address box and press Enter.

2. On the Trade Show Central home page, click the icon that says Trade Show Directory (see Figure 17.2).

3. On the next page, you'll see the Trade Show Central Search Utility (see Figure 17.3). It helps you find shows by name, industry category, date, city, or country.

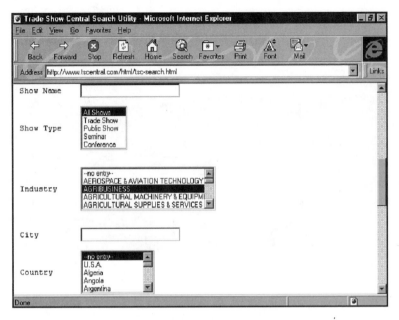

FIGURE 17.3    The Trade Show Central Search Utility lets you use scrollboxes to find specific types of shows.

4.   The Search Utility also lets you specify how you want your results sorted: by event name, city, country, or date.

5.   After you make your selections, click the Do Search button near the bottom of the page.

6.   You'll receive a table showing the location and date of the shows matching your search criteria. For additional details on a particular show, click its name.

7.   If you want more information than Trade Show Central provides, click the text at the top of the page that says **Request more information on this show.**

8.   You'll receive an electronic form. Fill it in and click the Send Request button near the bottom of the page. Your request will be forwarded to the trade show organizer who will send you additional details.

Trade Show Central offers several other features that business people may find useful. Look for these menu items on the site's home page (see Figure 17.2):

- **New Trade Show Profiles**  Detailed information on the latest entries in the database.

- **For Trade Show Organizers**  Information about putting your show in the database and letting Trade Show Central design a Web page for your event.

- **For Trade Show Exhibitors**  Information on advertising with Trade Show Central.

- **Strategic Marketing**  Links to companies that provide trade show marketing and survey services.

- **Exhibit Services Directory**  A database of information on more than 5,000 exhibit service vendors.

- **Venues & Facilities**  A database of information on more than 2,000 facilities worldwide, including arenas, amphitheaters, auditoriums, convention centers, hotels, theaters, and stadiums.

# OTHER BUSINESS TRAVEL RESOURCES

Here's a brief guide to other Web sites designed specifically for business travelers:

- EXPOguide (**http://www.expoguide.com/**) is another Web site with a trade show database. EXPOguide contains information on about 6,000 shows and also offers features that may be useful for meeting planners.

- Business Traveler (**http://www.btonline.com/**) is an electronic magazine offering travel news, details on bargains, investigative reports, and information on the world's major business cities. You can choose a U.S., U.K., or German edition of the online publication.

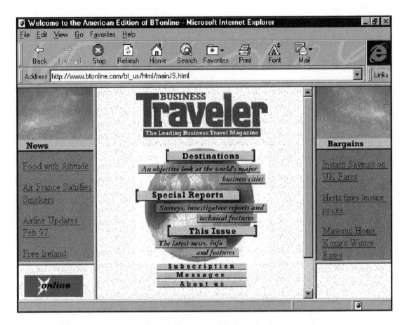

**FIGURE 17.4** Business Traveler is an online magazine with information on destinations and travel bargains.

- The software company Quicken sells ExpensAble, an expense report program. For information, visit **http://www.intuit.com/expensable/.**

- AT&T offers Business Traveler (**http://www.att.com/business/bustravel/index.html**). It includes a directory of links to international information, car rentals, travel agencies, restaurants, and airlines.

- The Business Traveler Info Network (**http://www.ultranet.com/~mes/biztrav.htm**) is a directory covering airlines, car rentals, hotels, overnight package delivery services, periodicals, software, and weather.

- Landseer Online (**http://www.landseer.com/**) is a directory that focuses on international business travel. You also will find an online message center where you can seek advice from other travelers.

In this lesson, you learned how to use online resources for business travelers. In the next lesson, you'll learn how to find hints for honeymooners.

# FINDING HINTS FOR HONEYMOONERS

*In this lesson, you'll learn how to use online resources that can help you plan a romantic trip.*

## A HELPING HAND AT HONEYMOONS.COM

Hiring a photographer, deciding on the music, finding the perfect dress or tuxedo, selecting a caterer—if you're planning a wedding, you know there are hundreds of details to take care of. You can always use a helping hand. The Web can provide it, especially when it comes to the honeymoon.

For example, look for the following features at Honeymoons.com (**http://www.honeymoons.com**):

- **Honeymoon Tips** offers advice on everything from planning a trip to checking your hotel room when you arrive.

- **Contest** includes quarterly drawings that could be your ticket to a free honeymoon in a romantic spot. You can register online.

- **Destinations** contains brief information on romantic places in the U.S., Caribbean, and Mexico.

- **Services** contains miscellaneous information.

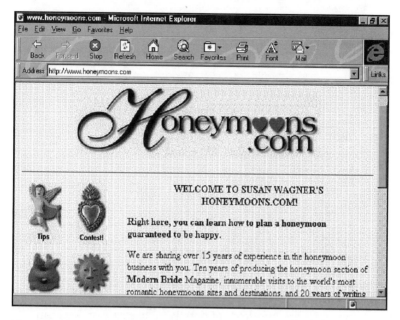

**FIGURE 18.1**   Honeymoon.com offers helpful hints.

# GETTING ADVICE ON ROMANTIC GETAWAYS

The Epicurious site described in Lesson 16, "Reading Electronic Travel Publications," offers a special section called Romantic Getaways. It features articles from *Bride's Magazine* as well as answers to readers' questions.

To access the Romantic Getaways section, you can use the site's main address (**http://travel.epicurious.com**), click the Places icon, and then select Romantic Getaways. Or you can go directly to the page with the URL:

**http://travel.epicurious.com/travel/b_places/ 01_romantic/intro.html.**

**FIGURE 18.2** Epicurious and *Bride's Magazine* team up to cover Romantic Getaways.

When you get there, you can access *Bride's* articles in any of the "for two" areas: "Caribbean for two," "U.S. and Hawaii for two," and "The World for two." For example, if you click the Caribbean for two icon, you'll be able to read such articles as Resorts of the U.S. Virgin Islands and The Essential Jamaica by clicking their titles.

The "U.S. and Hawaii for two" area contains articles such as "America's Great City Retreats," "America's Island Idylls," and "Hawaiian-Style Weddings." The "World for two" area features such titles as "Dream Trips at Real Prices," "A Taste for the Exotic," and "The Most Romantic Places on Earth."

The Q&A section contains readers' queries dating from June 1995. To see an answer, just click a question (see Figure 18.3).

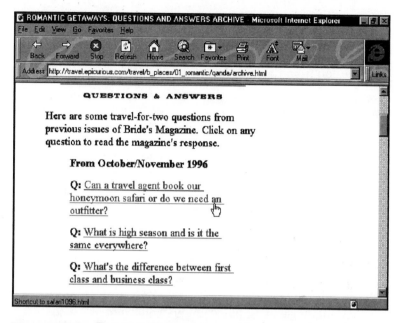

**FIGURE 18.3**    Romantic Getaways provides answers to honey-moon questions.

# OTHER HONEYMOON RESOURCES

Here are the Web addresses of several other honeymoon sites that may help you plan a romantic trip.

- Island Honeymoons is a site (**http://www.islandhoneymoons.com/**) sponsored by a travel agency that specializes in romantic journeys. Look in the Honeymoon Planning section for information on the Honeymoon Registry Program.

- Honeymoon Travel (**http://www.honeymoontravel.com/**), specializes in Caribbean, all-inclusive honeymoons. An all-inclusive honeymoon includes everything in one price.

- My Wedding Companion (**http://users.southeast. net/~fivestar/index.html**) offers wedding planning software for Windows. You can download a shareware version from the Web site.

- BridalNet (**http://www.bridalnet.com**) includes a Honeymoon section with links to many different travel agencies.

- America Online offers honeymoon resources in its own online area called The Knot (keyword: **knot**). You can find ideas and destination information in the section called **The Great Escape**. Also look for the **Honeymoon Talk** and **Travel Tips** forum in the message boards area.

- The Honeymoon Travel Specials section of World Wide Weddings (**http://www.worldwideweddings.com/**) includes information on cruises, island destinations, mountain getaways, and "unique honeymoons." Also look for details on the Honeymoon Bridal Registry.

- Honeymoon Cruise Source (**http://www.tiac.net/ vacation/wedding/**) is an agency that can help you book a boat trip. You can also register to receive information on weekly cruise specials via e-mail.

- If you're interested in a "Fairy Tale Wedding" or honeymoon at Disney World, take a trip to the Web page **http://www.disney.com/DisneyWorld/Resorts/ index.html**. Scroll to the bottom of the page and click the Fairy Tale Wedding link. It will take you to the page shown in part in Figure 18.4. If you're only interested in honeymoon information, scroll to the bottom of the wedding page and click the Honeymoon link. See Lesson 20, "Visiting Amusement Parks," for more information about the Disney World Web site.

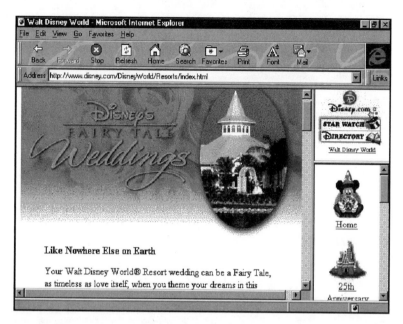

**FIGURE 18.4** Check into the Disney World site for information on fairy tale weddings and honeymoons.

In this lesson, you learned how to find hints for honeymooners. In the next lesson, you'll learn how to explore adventure and recreation travel.

# 19

# EXPLORING ADVENTURE AND RECREATION TRAVEL

*In this lesson, you'll learn how to find adventure vacations as well as golf and ski resorts.*

## SEARCHING FOR ADVENTURE

Biking, hiking, climbing, canoeing, diving, safaris, dude ranches... If you enjoy any of those activities, you may be looking for an adventure vacation.

A Web site that can help you find a fun adventure is called Action Trips. It provides an online directory you can use to look for trips offered by 164 tour operators worldwide.

You can search for adventures in thirteen categories. Besides the ones mentioned above, you can find information on cultural expeditions, horseback riding, rafting, kayaking, sailing, research trips, and photography.

To use Action Trips, follow these steps:

1. Type the URL **http://www.actiontrips.com/** in your Web browser's location box and press Enter.

2. Scroll down the home page. You'll see icons representing different types of adventures (one is shown in Figure 19.1). Click the icon for the type of trip you want.

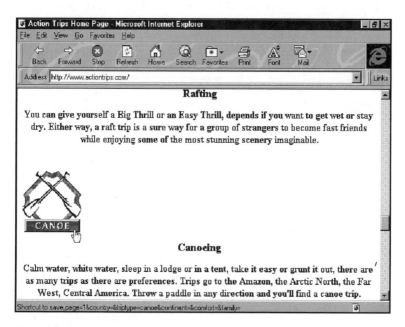

**FIGURE 19.1**   Choose an adventure at Action Trips.

3. The next page presents an interactive world map. Click the continent where you want to go.

4. Select a country in the Country/State scrollbox (see Figure 19.2). If you clicked North America in the last step, you can choose a specific U.S. state or Canadian province.

5. In the Comfort box select either Comfortable Wilderness or Safe Thrills. As the page notes, Comfortable Wilderness includes a bed, hot water, and meal service. Safe Thrills means participatory camping, which includes sleeping bags.

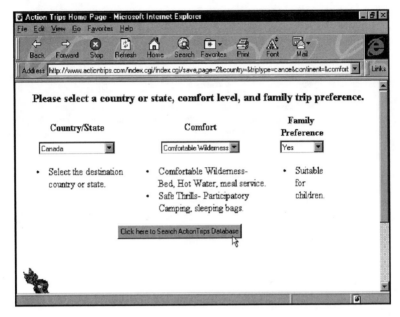

FIGURE 19.2    The Web site lets you specify the type of trip you're seeking.

6. In the family preference box, select Yes if you're looking for trips where you can take children along. Choose No if you're not.

7. After you've made your selections, click the button Click Here to Search Action Trips Database.

8. Your search results will include a table of information. If you want to visit a Web site for a particular adventure provider, click the Goto Site link in the URL column (see Figure 19.3).

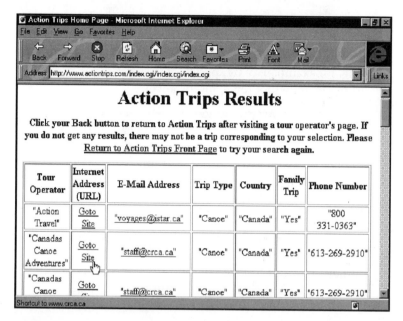

**FIGURE 19.3**   Action Trips provides detailed information on adventure tour providers.

## MORE ADVENTURE GUIDES

Here's a sampling of several other adventure directories you can access on the Web:

- Adventure Tour Directory (**http://www. adventuretours.com/trips**) offers information on activities ranging from "soft adventure" to whitewater rafting.

- Safari Adventure Travel Directory (**http://www.laig. com/safari**) is a list of tour guides, tour operators, and travel agencies that provide safari and adventure trips.

- Active and Adventurous Travel (**http://www.gorp. com/gorp/trips/main.htm**) helps you find information by location, by activity (hiking, biking, birding, fishing, for example), or by special interest (archaeology, ecotourism, senior tours, for instance).

- Travel Source (**http://www.travelsource.com**) offers information on more than forty tour operators specializing in such adventures as safaris, wine tours, cycling, villa rentals, trekking, spas, rafting, yachting, scuba diving, and much more. Part of the Travel Source directory is shown in Figure 10.3 at the end of Lesson 10, "Finding Online Travel Agents and Tour Operators".

- Special Interest Travel Consult'ium (**http://sitravel. com**) provides information in several interesting and unique tour categories, including architecture, choir, culinary, disabled, diving, heritage, history, wellness, and music. There's even a separate category for opera tours.

## FINDING GOLF AND SKI INFORMATION

Whether you want to hit the slopes or the greens, the Web can help you find a resort. The Epicurious site described in Lesson 16, "Reading Electronic Travel Publications," provides innovative features that can help you find golf or ski resorts worldwide. You can search for them by the features most important to you. Here's how:

1. Type the URL **http://travel.epicurious.com/** in your Web browser's location box and press Enter.

2. Scroll to the bottom of the home page and click the Search button in the menubar.

3. On the next page click either Find a Ski Resort or Find a Golf Resort. The golf search engine contains information on fifty resorts; the ski feature covers 160.

4. Whichever search engine you choose, you'll see a box that lets you select how important you consider certain features (see Figure 19.4). After you make your selections in the scrollboxes, click the button Show my personalized resort rankings.

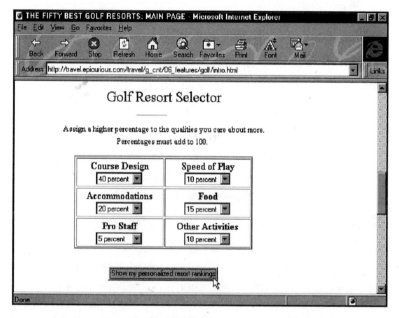

FIGURE 19.4   Epicurious helps you find resorts with the features most important to you.

5. Your search results will include a list of resorts ranked according to the selections you made. Click a resort's name to get more information about it.

6. If you use the Back button on your browser to return to the main golf or ski search page, you can scroll down below the table shown in Figure 19.4 to access lists of the top resorts in each of the ranking categories.

## OTHER GOLF AND SKI DIRECTORIES

- Golf Web (**http://www.golfweb.com/**) provides OnCourse, which it bills as "The Largest Golf Course Database on the Internet." It covers over 20,000 courses in seven countries. You also can find more than 7,000 reader comments.

- Global Golf (**http://www.globalgolf.com/**) provides a destination guide for PGA European Tour events. You'll find information on where to play, stay, and dine.

- Yahoo! offers an extensive list of links to golf-related information. Starting on the site's home page (**http://www.yahoo.com**), select the following categories: Business and Economy, Companies, Sports, and Golf. Then you may want to select Courses, Tour Operators, or Country Clubs and Resorts.

- The Best Ski Resorts! (**http://www.excitement.com/ski/ski1.htm**) lets you search specific states and a few European countries. You also can find snowboarding information.

- Hyperski: Resorts (**http://www.hyperski.com/resorts/resorts100.htm**) promises to provide snow conditions for every U.S. ski resort. In addition, you can find information on resorts in Canada, Europe, Asia, and New Zealand.

- Yahoo! offers links to numerous ski areas. You even can find a directory of other ski directories. Go to **http://www.yahoo.com** and select the categories Business and Economy, Companies, Sports, and Skiing. Then select either Ski Areas or Tour Operators.

In this lesson, you learned how to find details on adventure and recreation travel. In the next lesson, you'll learn how to find information on amusement parks.

# VISITING ONLINE AMUSEMENT PARKS

*In this lesson, you'll learn how to find information about Disneyland, Walt Disney World, and other theme parks.*

## ACCESSING DISNEY ONLINE

If you're heading for Disneyland or Walt Disney World, you first may want to head to the online versions of the Magical Kingdoms. The theme parks' Web sites are more than just electronic brochures. They also offer travel tips, lodging recommendations, general park information, schedules, and details on rides and events.

Disney has many technically adept fans, and some of them have created their own unofficial Web pages. For example, one is available from Jeff Keller, a college student majoring in cognitive science and dreaming of becoming a Disney Imagineer. Keller's Disneyland page:

**http://lostworld.pair.com/disneyland/disneyland.html**

It includes an interactive map, ride reviews, digital photos, and details on tickets and hours of operation.

Another fan has created a Web site called The Official Disneyland Ride Lyric Database:

**http://www.interactive.net/~imperia/disney.html**

Visit it if you really want to know the words to the music you hear in attractions such as The Pirates of the Caribbean or The Enchanted Tiki Room.

To access the official Disneyland page, go to Disney's main site (**http://www.disney.com**). It covers the theme parks as well as Disney movies, books, television, theater, shopping, and software. Click the word Disneyland under the Theme Parks/Vacations heading. To directly access the Disneyland site (shown in part in Figure 20.1), you can use the URL **http://www.disney.com/ Disneyland/**.

**FIGURE 20.1**    Visit Disneyland online if you're headed for the real thing.

Here's a quick tour of several areas of the official Disneyland site:

- **What's New?** is the place to look for information on new rides and attractions.

- **Park Information** provides basic details on events, hours, and ticket prices. You also can find an online map and information on local weather and traffic. You even can find directions to the park from local freeways.

- **Magical Places to Stay** includes information on the Disneyland Hotel as well as special packages and promotions.

- **Tour Guides** are virtual tours of the Magic Kingdom.

- **Travel Information** offers details on packages available from the Walt Disney Travel Company as well as links to the other areas of the site with travel information.

## THE VIRTUAL WALT DISNEY WORLD

If you want information on Walt Disney World, either select it from Disney's home page or use the URL:

**http://www.disney.com/Walt Disney World/index.html.**

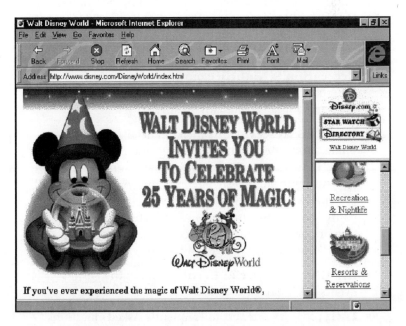

**FIGURE 20.2**    Walt Disney World's Web page is a high-tech guide to the park.

Look for the following features on the Walt Disney World Page. You can select them from the frame on the right side of the screen (see Figure 20.2):

- **Theme Parks, Maps & Live Cameras** provides basic information on tickets and hours of operation as well as several innovative features. For example, in the sections for the Magic Kingdom, Epcot, and Disney-MGM Studios, you can search for specific types of information such as rides for particular age groups. You also can find information on dining options and download highly detailed maps. They're available in the Portable Document Format explained in Lesson 6, "Storing the Information You Find." You can see panoramic images in the QuickTime VR format. (You can download a QuickTime VR player through the Disney site. For more information about QuickTime, see the note at the end of Lesson 23, "Taking Virtual Vacations".) Images from live cameras in the theme parks are available, too.

- **Recreation & Nightlife** provides information on waterparks, fishing, golf, tennis, shopping, health clubs, programs for kids, and baby-sitting.

- **Resorts & Reservations** includes details on Disney's Value, Moderate, Deluxe, Camping, and Home Away from Home resorts. You can fill out and submit an online reservation form. A Disney reservation counselor will call or e-mail you in twenty-four to seventy-two hours to finalize the details. Also look in this section for information on having a Fairy Tale Wedding or honeymoon at Walt Disney World.

- **Highlights & Special Events** includes the Disney Events Calendar.

- **FAQs** provides Answers to Frequently Asked Questions about Walt Disney World.

- **Disabled Guest Information** includes information for visitors who have sight, mobility, or hearing disabilities.

## DISCOVERING THE DISNEY INSTITUTE

You can find information on The Disney Institute either through
a link on the Walt Disney World Page or through Disney's home
page. Disney describes its institute as "a whole new Disney vacation experience. A resort community with a campus-like setting,
the Disney Institute offers more than 40 hands-on programs and
activities taught in a relaxed, social atmosphere by fun-loving
instructors who are experts in their fields."

Those fields include Design Arts, Culinary Arts, Sports & Fitness,
Performing Arts & Film, Lifestyles, Story Arts, Youth Programs,
Entertainment Arts, and Gardening & Great Outdoors. You can
find information about all the activities and vacation packages
online (see Figure 20.3).

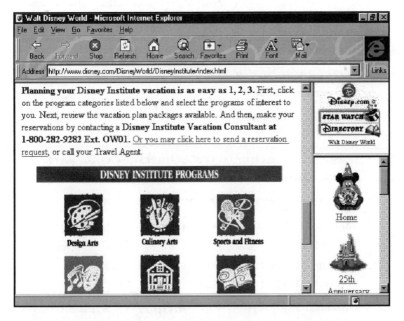

FIGURE 20.3   The Disney Institute is "a whole new Disney
Vacation experience."

## DISNEY AROUND THE WORLD

The Web site for Disneyland Paris is available at **http://www. disney.fr/dlp/**. At this writing the site is still under construction, but the builders promise to add several features that will help you plan a trip. You also will be able to choose an English or French version.

You can choose an English or Japanese version of the Walt Disney World Tokyo site (**http://www.tokyodisneyland.co.jp/**). Like the other Disney pages, the Tokyo site provides a detailed guide to the park's attractions and events.

# OTHER THEME PARK SITES

Here are the Web addresses of other popular theme parks in the U.S. Most of them provide detailed information that can help you plan a trip:

- Anheuser-Busch Theme Parks, such as Busch Gardens and Sea World, are accessible through **http://www. 4adventure.com/**

- Coney Island—**http://www.brooklynonline.com/ coneyisland/**

- Hersheypark—**http://www.800hershey.com/park/ index.html**

- Knott's Berry Farm—**http://www.knotts.com/**

- Paramount's Great American and Kings Island—**http:// www.pki.com/**

- Six Flags Theme Parks (all twelve of them)—**http:// www.sixflags.com/**

- Universal Studios Hollywood—**http://www.mca.com/ unicity/**

- Universal Studios Florida—**http://www.usf.com/**

- A directory to both official and unofficial theme park sites is available at **http://www.mcs.net/~werner/ parklinks.html**. That page is part of Yesterland (**http:/ /www.mcs.net/~werner/yester.html**), a site about discontinued Disneyland Attractions.

- Yahoo! offers an extensive directory of theme park and related sites (see Figure 20.4). Visit **http://www.yahoo. com**, choose the category Entertainment, and then the category Amusement/Theme Parks.

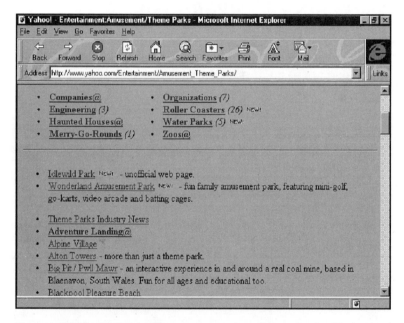

**FIGURE 20.4**   Yahoo! offers an extensive directory of online amusement parks.

In this lesson, you learned how to find information about amusement parks. In the next lesson, you'll learn how to explore camping in cyberspace.

# CAMPING IN CYBERSPACE

*In this lesson, you'll learn how to use online camping resources.*

## SEARCHING CAMPGROUND DIRECTORIES

If you're a camping enthusiast, you're probably used to roughing it. You don't need mints on your pillow, linen and crystal on your table, or any other fancy frills. Well, have I got a Web site for you.

**Benz's Campground Directory** bills itself as "a simple directory without a lot of fancy graphics." But it does offer extensive lists of campgrounds and RV parks across the U.S. and Canada. To use the directory, just follow these steps:

1. Type the URL **http://www.cfw.com/~benz/ camp.htm** in your Web browser's location box and press Enter.

2. Scroll down the site's home page until you see the tables for U.S. and Canada (see Figure 21.1).

3. Click the name of the state or province you're interested in.

4. You'll receive a list of campgrounds organized by city. The list includes telephone numbers and, when available, links to Web sites and e-mail addresses. Just click a link to visit the site or send e-mail.

**FIGURE 21.1** Benz's Campground Directory provides extensive lists of campgrounds in the U.S. and (not shown) Canada.

A camping site with a few fancier features (including a Let's Talk Camping Forum) as well as a database that offers sophisticated search options is available at Holiday Internet Connections Campground Directory. It provides details on more than 10,000 U.S. campgrounds. To search the database, follow these steps:

1. Type the URL **http://www.rving.com/** in your Web browser's location box and press Enter.

2. Click the Enter Here link at the bottom of the page.

3. Click the Search button in the menu bar.

4. The next page (shown in part in Figure 21.2) lets you select several criteria to narrow your search for a particular type of campground. Make your selections by clicking the checkboxes.

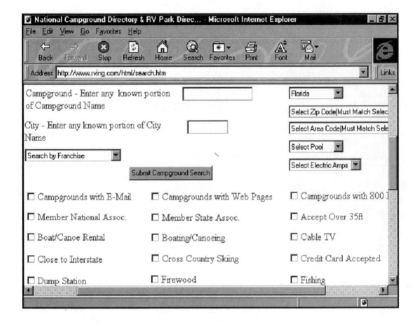

**FIGURE 21.2** Holiday Internet Connections' Campground Directory lets you use several search criteria.

5. Click one of the two Submit Campground Search buttons. They're located near the top and bottom of the page.

6. Your search results will include a list of the campgrounds matching your criteria. Click the name of a campground for more information.

# MAKING KOA RESERVATIONS

Kampgrounds of America offers an online directory of KOA facilities in the U.S., Canada, Mexico, and Japan. You can use it to find information on making reservations with any individual campground. Here's how:

1. Type the URL **http://www.koakampgrounds.com** in your Web browser's location box and press Enter.

2. Click the Where are KAOs link beneath the picture on the home page (see Figure 21.3).

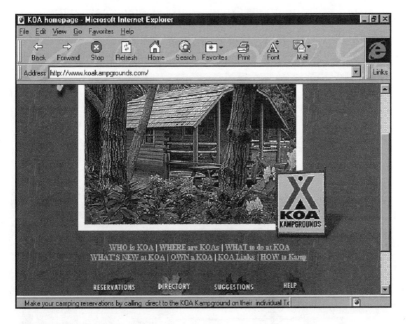

**FIGURE 21.3**   KOA's Web site can help you find reservation numbers for "Kampgrounds" in the U.S., Canada, Mexico, and Japan.

3. Near the bottom of the next page, select a state, province, or country in the scrollbox.

4. Click the GO! button.

5. You'll receive a list of cities or regions in the appropriate area. Click the one you're interested in. If you started on the country level, you may receive another list of geographic areas to choose from.

6. When you narrow your choice to a specific location and campground, you'll receive a description, a list of amenities, and rate information (Figure 21.4 shows part of a page for an individual campground). Write down the phone number at the top of the screen or save it using one of the methods explained in Lesson 6, "Saving the Information You Find." Call the number to make a reservation directly with the campground.

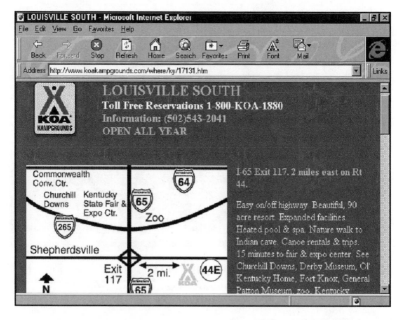

**Figure 21.4**   KOA offers detailed information on individual campgrounds.

7. If you want information on KOA's reservation procedures, use the Back button on your browser to return to KOA's home page.

8. Near the bottom, click the Reservations button (see Figure 21.3).

9. Click Reservations and Cancellation Procedures.

# OTHER CAMPING RESOURCES

Here are the Web addresses of several other useful camping sites:

- Yahoo! offers a directory to online resources in such categories as Camping Gear, Commercial and Summer Camps, Food, Hiking Tour Operators, and RV Parks and Campgrounds. Use the URL **http://www.yahoo.com/** and then select the categories: Business and Economy, Companies, Outdoors, Camping.

- The National Park Service offers Parknet (**http://www. nps.gov/**). It contains destination, nature, and general information.

- The North American Holiday Guide (**http://www. holidayguide.com/**) offers directories of campgrounds, RV parks, marinas, charters, and condominium rentals.

- CampNet America (**http://www.kiz.com**) offers an RV Parks and Campgrounds Locator as well as links to national and public park information. You also can find lists of RV and tent manufacturers, travel clubs, camping associations, equipment suppliers, and more.

## ON THE ROAD RESOURCES

The resources listed above can help you find camping destinations; the sites listed below can help you plan your trips to them:

- Delorme offers the online CyberRouter (**http://route. delorme.com/**). You can use it to generate maps and driving instructions between more than 240,000 places in the U.S. The CyberRouter page also includes a link to a CyberAtlas (see also Lesson 11, "Generating Online Maps").

- AutoPilot (**http://www.freetrip.com/**) offers an online Highway Trip Planning System. You can use it to create personalized itineraries that include the locations of restaurants, national parks, and other facilities along your route. You also can choose direct or scenic routes and plan a trip that avoids toll roads.

- Rand McNally Online (**http://www.randmcnally. com**) provides a database of information on road construction. Look for it in the Web site's travel tools section.

In this lesson, you learned about online camping resources. In the next lesson, you'll learn how to find hostel information.

# FINDING HOSTEL INFORMATION

*In this lesson, you'll learn how to find and use online hostel resources.*

## EXPLORING THE WORLD OF HOSTELLING

Hostelling is "often referred to as backpacking in many parts of the world, and it's perhaps best described as traveling cheaply with an adventurous spirit."

That's a definition from the Internet Guide to Hostelling, which also notes that "while hostelling, you see the world from a perspective that the average tourist will never see. You meet local people, learn customs, eat local food, and often have opportunities to do things you never imagined."

The Internet Guide to Hostelling is a Web site offering several online resources for people interested in exploring the world of hostelling. For example, it provides an electronic directory to thousands of hostels in more than 150 regions. To use the guide, follow these steps:

1. Type the URL **http://www.hostels.com/** in your Web browser's location box and press Enter.

2. On the home page, click the The Worldwide Hostel Guide link (see Figure 22.1).

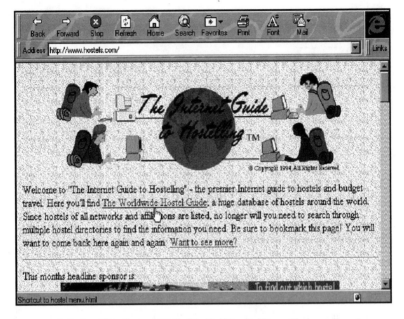

**FIGURE 22.1** The Internet Guide to Hostelling offers a directory to hostels in over 150 world regions.

3. On the next page, choose an area of the world under the **Where do you want to go?** heading.

4. The next page lets you select the country you're interested in. Just click the name.

5. You'll receive a list of hostels in that country. Figure 22.2 shows part of the page for hostels in England. Please note that the hostel lists tend to be extremely long pages and may take a few minutes to completely download to your Web browser.

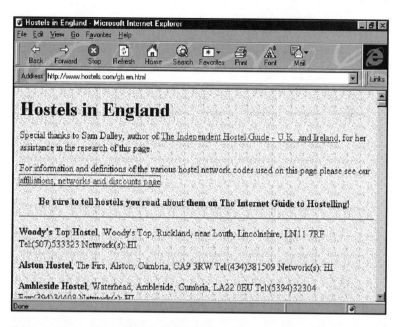

**FIGURE 22.2** The Worldwide Hostel Guide lists hostels by country.

**TIP**

**Searching an Individual Web Page** As mentioned above, the hostel listings can be very long Web pages, but you may not have to read the whole list. Most Web browsers let you search the page for individual words and phrases. Click Edit on the browser's menu bar, and then click the text that says Find on This Page. A window will open, and you can type in the word or phrase you want to find on the Web page you're viewing. If you're searching the Hostels in England page for accommodations in, say, East Sussex, just search for those words and your browser will jump to the first mention of it on the page. Click Find Next to jump to subsequent references.

# OTHER HOSTEL FEATURES

Other features available through the Internet Guide to Hostelling include:

- **Frequently Asked Questions about Hostelling** provides answers to such common queries as "What are hostels?", "Who stays there?", "What documents do I need?", "What is the atmosphere like?", and "What equipment do I need?"

- **What's "News" in Hostelling** includes information on new hostels and discounts for backpackers.

- **Ski Country Hostels** is a directory of accommodations near ski areas in the U.S. and Canada (part of the page is shown in Figure 22.3). At this writing, the site's developers plan to add information on hostels near ski areas in other areas of the world.

**FIGURE 22.3**    Ski Country Hostels is a guide to lodging near U.S. and Canadian ski areas for about $20 or less per night.

- **The Guide to Budget Guidebooks** provides reviews of publications that include hostel information.

- **Going Places** includes information on such topics as "Exciting Backpacker Bus Adventures", "Save with Air Passes", "Budget Travel in North America", "Drive Someone Else's Car—For Free!", "The Art of Renting a Car—Cheaply", and "Buy a Car Now and Sell it Later."

- **The Hosteler's Virtual Bulletin Board** is the place to post electronic notes if you want to find travel companions, rides, equipment, and information on virtually any other hostelling topic.

## MORE HOSTEL RESOURCES

The Internet Guide to Hostelling also offers a section of Links to Other Hostel Resources on the Net. The links are organized into several categories: Other Hostelling Pages, Individual Hostel Home Pages, and Other Internet Budget Travel Resources. Here's a sampling of the site's you can find:

- Hostels Europe  **http://www.eurotrip.com/**

- Russian Youth Hostels  **http://www.spb.su/ryh/home.html**

- Budget Backpackers Hostel New Zealand  **http://www.backpack.co.nz/**

- Austrian Youth Hostelling Federation  **http://www.cso.co.at/oejhw/**

- Global Passage  **http://www.globalpassage.com/** (See Lesson 16, "Reading Electronic Travel Publications.")

In this lesson, you learned how to find hostel information. In the next lesson, you'll learn how to vacation in cyberspace.

# GOING ON VIRTUAL VACATIONS

*In this lesson, you'll learn how to take a trip on the Web.*

## TAKING A TERRAQUEST

If you don't have the time or money for your dream vacation, cyberspace is the place to go instead.

The Web is a powerful vehicle for armchair adventurers. Vivid writing combined with digital images, online audio, video, live cameras, virtual reality, and other Internet technologies can take you to exotic places around the world.

Some of the technologies require special software and long download times (see the list of sites with video at the end of this lesson), and your trip will be more pleasant if you have access to a fast Internet connection, such as ISDN or a high-speed link like many corporations use.

Other sites provide pretty good virtual expeditions through modems operating at speeds as low as 28,800 bps. For example, a Web site called TerraQuest provides several high-quality and high-tech travelogues that do not take an especially long time to appear on your screen.

At this writing, TerraQuest lets you choose from three adventures:

- **Climbing into History** takes you 3,000 feet up the face of El Capitan! in Yosemite National Park.

- **Head for Virtual Galápagos** explores the "living laboratory of evolution."

- **Going' South**  Way South is an Antarctica expedition.

To illustrate the type of information available through TerraQuest, this lesson focuses on the digital Galápagos. To begin the adventure, just select Head for Virtual Galápagos! (see Figure 23.1) from the site's Home Page (**http://www.terraquest.com**).

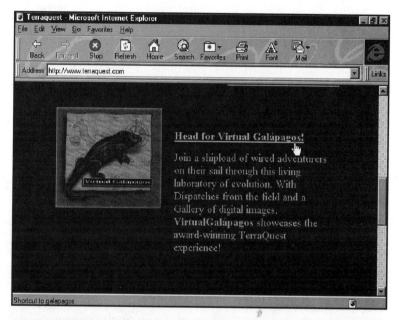

**FIGURE 23.1**    TerraQuest lets you surf to the Galápagos via modem.

After you enter the virtual Galápagos you can choose from several features:

- The Gallery offers more than 20 digital images, including pictures of a blue-footed booby bird and a giant tortoise (see Figure 23.2).

- The QTVR Gallery includes five videos in the QuickTime format (see the note about QuickTime in the last section of this lesson).

- The Atlas includes interactive maps that chart the Galápagos and the mainland of Ecuador. You also can find a few QuickTime videos here.

- Dispatches are notes from the field written by the Terra-Quest exploration team. This section also contains some interesting digital images.

- Expedition includes Terra-Team profiles, ship specifications, rules for eco-tourism, and an invitation to join the team on their next adventure.

- History lets you learn about the pirates, naval captains, naturalists, conquistadors, and liberators who have visited the Galápagos.

- Issues explores environmental problems confronting the islands.

- Wildlife provides images and information on the area's land and marine life. You also can access a checklist of species.

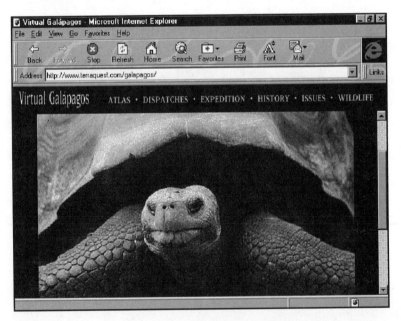

FIGURE 23.2  A giant tortoise is just one of the species you'll spot on your virtual tour.

# More Virtual Vacations

Here are several more sites for armchair adventurers. The first few are sites that work fairly well with modems operating at speeds as low as 28.8 kbps. The next section notes sites featuring Webcam images. It may take a few minutes to download them at 28.8. The last section lists sites featuring online video or virtual reality technology. Those sites may require special software and the images can take several minutes to download.

- Cyber Adventures (**http://www.cyber-adv.com/**) lets you track explorers and vacationers. Also look for The Coolest Travel Site of the Week and Strange (But True) Travel Stories.

- Virtual Tours (**http://www.dreamscape.com/ frankvad/tours.html**) provides links to online tours through more than 150 museums and exhibits, over 100 cities and countries, and several U.S. government sites, including the White House.

- The Adventure Channel (**http://www.180.com/**) lets you follow explorers' exploits. For example, in Running the Nile, you can learn about a team of kayakers who attempted a "first ever" descent of the Victoria Nile River in Uganda, Africa.

- Virtual Expeditions (**http://www.coil.com/ ~jhegenbe/virtex.htm**) is a directory that offers a "list of Web sites that involve Travelogues and Dispatches that take you on personal journeys to almost any destination in the world."

- Look for many more virtual vacation spots at Yahoo! (**http://www.yahoo.com**). Starting on the Home Page, select the following categories: Recreation, Travel, Travelogues.

**FIGURE 23.3**    Follow explorers' exploits with The Adventure Channel.

## WEBCAMS

The following sites show live images from various locations.

> **Webcam**   A camera, usually set up in a permanent location, that sends frequently updated images to the Web.

- Mt. Fuji Viewer (**http://www.city.fujiyoshida. yamanashi.jp/mtfuji/tonbo/index-e.html**) lets you view Mt. Fuji and "move the camera yourself."

- The Manhattan Skyline Webcam (**http://www. realtech.com/webcam/index.htm**) is live from the seventy-seventh floor of the Empire State Building. Also look for links to time-lapse photography, city guides, links to other New York Webcams, and general Webcam directories.

**FIGURE 23.4**    Manhattan via a Webcam on the Empire State
Building.

- Mawson Station, Antarctica (**http://www.antdiv.
  gov.au/aad/exop/sfo/mawson/video.html**) includes an image, updated every hour, that is captured at
  the station and sent via a permanent satellite link to the
  Australian Antarctic Division's Headquarters at Kingston,
  Tasmania, where it is put on the Web.

- Polo Towers Webcam Las Vegas (**http://www.
  polotowers.com/**) is located next to the MGM. This
  Webcam usually does a continuous sweep of the Las Vegas strip and randomly snaps a picture every five minutes.
  Also look for the panoramic view of Vegas.

- EarthCam (**http://www.earthcam.com/**) is a directory of other Webcam sites on the Internet. You can
  browse by category or geographic region.

## VIDEO AND VIRTUAL REALITY SPOTS

Most of the following Web sites offer QuickTime videos. To play them you need a copy of the QuickTime software installed on your computer. QuickTime is available for Mac, OS and Windows 3.1, 95, and NT. You can download a copy through links in the following Web sites, or you can go directly to the QuickTime Home Page (**http://qtvr.quicktime.apple.com**).

Some of these sites also offer video in other formats such as AVI, which can be played with the Media Player that comes with Windows 95. As mentioned earlier, videos can take several minutes to download to your computer.

- Vancouver VR (**http://www2.portal.ca/ ~raymondk/Spider/movies.html**) provides a virtual tour of Vancouver, British Columbia, Canada.

- Scenes of the Lake Atitlán Area in Guatemala (**http:// www.mecc.com/MAYA/QTVR/Lake.Atitlan/ Lake.Atitlan.QTVR.html**) is part of MayaQuest (**http://www.mecc.com/mayaquest.html**) a virtual expedition to "the lost cities of the rain forest."

- TASC offers virtual flyovers of three-dimensional, synthetic terrain (**http://www.tasc.com/fun/3d.html**). The Face on Mars and Yellowstone National Park on Fire videos are available in QuickTime as well as the AVI and MPEG formats.

- British Airways Gallery (**http://www.britishairways. com/inside/media/gallery/gallery.shtml**) offers a virtual reality tour of the inside of a first class cabin. Footage of the Concord in flight is available in QuickTime and the AVI format. Images of all the planes in the British Airways fleet are available, too.

- DesertUSA (**http://www.desertusa.com/**) offers virtual tours of several national parks, including the Grand Canyon.

- The Tampa/Hillsborough (Florida) Convention and Visitors Association's web site offers a QuickTime ride on Busch Garden's Montu, the world's largest inverted steel roller coaster (**http://www.thcva.com/demo.htm**).

- Planet 9 Studios (**http://www.planet9.com/**) provides 3D tours of several cities, including San Diego, Manhattan, Washington, D.C., and Las Vegas. The tours are available in VRML. To find out how to use that format, click the link How To View 3D Worlds on the site's Home Page.

 **VRML**   An acronym (pronounced "ver-mul") for Virtual Reality Modeling Language, a protocol for creating interactive, three-dimensional features on Web sites.

In this lesson, you learned how to take virtual vacations. In the next lesson, you'll learn how to use resources that can help you connect to the Internet when you're on the road.

# 24 TRAVEL RESOURCES FOR MOBILE NET USERS

*In this lesson, you'll learn how to find world phone guides, directories of Internet cafés, and other resources that can help you stay connected when you're traveling.*

## LOGGING ON FROM ALMOST ANYWHERE

Just because you're out of town doesn't mean you have to give up your Internet travels. A laptop computer with a modem and the resources listed here can help you stay in touch.

For example, the World Wide Phone Guide addresses "what you need to hook up your modem just about anywhere!" The site includes a table of telephone plugs used worldwide and offers detailed instructions for handling hard-wired phone systems, using an acoustic coupler, basic wiretapping, and special situations such as digital phones and tax impulses (high-frequency pulse signals used in some countries to meter phone usage).

To find out which type of phone plug you need for a specific country, follow these steps:

1. Type the URL **http://www.cris.com/~kropla/ phones.htm** in your Web browser's location box and press Enter.

2. Click the text table of telephone plugs near the top of the home page.

3. Scroll down the table (shown in part in Figure 24.1) until you see the listing for the country you're interested in.

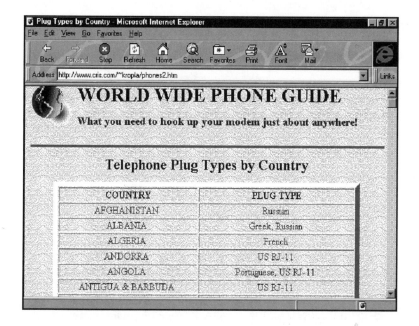

**FIGURE 24.1** The table of telephone plugs can help you find out how to connect to the Internet around the world.

4. Now that you know what type of plug you need, how do you get it? One way is to use the Back button on your browser to return to World Wide Phone Guide's main page. Then click the highlighted word sources in the first paragraph.

5. Now you'll see a list of equipment suppliers. For most of them, you can click the name to visit the Web site, and check to see if the supplier carries the type of plug you need.

# FINDING AN INTERNET CAFÉ

What if you want to be able to connect to the Internet while you travel, but you don't want to lug a laptop?

You can visit an Internet café. Available in many cities around the world, they offer computers and Internet connections for public use.

The Cyber Café Guide (**http://www.cyberiacafe.net/ cyberia/guide/ccafe.htm**) provides an extensive list of cafés worldwide, but at this writing, the site hasn't been updated in several months. So if you find a café you want to visit, first take a trip to its Web page to make sure it's still in business.

Another list of cafés and links to several other directories are available at Yahoo! To find them, follow these steps.

1. Type **http://www.yahoo.com** in your Web browser's location box and press Enter.

2. Starting on the site's home page, select the following categories: Society and Culture, Cyberculture, Internet Cafés.

3. You'll see a long list of cafés arranged alphabetically. Scroll down the list until you see one that look interesting. You also can search the list through the window near the top of the page. If you use a geographic name as your keyword, you may be able to find a café in a specific city, state, or country. The search engine may miss relevant sites, however, because not all the descriptions on the Yahoo! page include geographic names.

4. When you find a café that looks interesting, click the name to visit its Web site. Then use the Back button on your browser to return to the Yahoo! list.

5. Click the word Indices near the top of the page. You will see the list shown in Figure 24.2. Click the name of any index to access and use it.

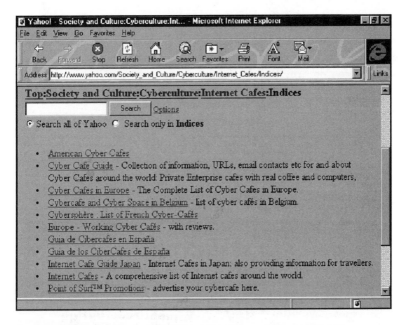

**FIGURE 24.2**  Yahoo! provides a directory of directories to Internet cafés.

**Searching Alphabetical Lists**  If the Internet café directory you're using offers only an alphabetical list of names (as American Cyber Cafés does), use the Find function in your browser's Edit menu to search for cafés in specific geographic locations. (For more information, see the tip in Lesson 22.)

# MORE RESOURCES FOR MOBILE NET USERS

Here's are notes on a few other sites that may be useful for "technomads":

- Walkabout Travel Gear (**http://www. walkabouttravelgear.com/**) is an online equipment supplier. You can order mobile computer and telecommunications equipment online. Walkabout also offers a great deal of basic information about computing and connecting to the Internet around the world.

- The MapQuest site (**http://www.mapquest.com**) lets you choose Internet cafés as Points of Interest. See Lesson 11, "Generating Online Maps" for more information about using MapQuest and identifying Points of Interest.

- Mobile Computing & Communications Magazine provides a Web site (**http://www.mobilecomputing. com/**) with news and online articles.

- PC LapTop magazine's site (**http://www2.pclaptop. com/pclaptop/**) includes articles as well as miscellaneous computer and Internet tips.

- TechnoTravel (**http://www2.dk-online.dk/users/ Anders_Andersen/**) offers links to many different resources for traveling online users. You can find information on global Internet providers, Web-based e-mail accounts, world electric and telephone plug guides, and even satellite communications sites that can help you stay in touch if you're "trekking the jungle of Borneo."

**FIGURE 24.3**    TechnoTravel is a valuable resource for "technomads."

In this lesson, you learned how to use resources for traveling online users. In the next lesson, you'll learn about the travel information available on America Online.

# FINDING TRAVEL INFORMATION ON AMERICA ONLINE

*In this lesson, you'll learn how to find and use America Online's travel resources.*

## WHAT TRAVEL INFORMATION DOES AOL OFFER?

America Online is an electronic community, an e-mail system, an Internet gateway, a live chat room host, and an information provider on topics ranging from setting up a Web site to buying a new car to cooking Spanish tapas.

AOL also offers many high-quality travel resources. In fact, it provides an entire "channel" of travel information, products, and services (see Figure 25.1). To access this area, just click the Travel button on the main channel screen. Or click the Keyword button on the menu bar, type in **travel**, and click the Go button.

The Travel Channel's Fantasize area is the place to visit for travel ideas. You can find information on specific types of travel, online publications, photos, and videos.

The Research & Plan area offers information on all fifty states as well as countries and cities around the world. Other features include foreign language information, maps, tips, and weather resources.

**FIGURE 25.1**   The AOL Travel channel offers easy access to all the online service's vacation and business trip resources.

The Travel channels Book It! area includes lodging guides, details on travel deals and links to Web sites for Amtrack reservations, Canadian and European Rail information, and Greyhound bus schedules. You also can access a travel club and make travel reservations online.

**Use the Find Button**   An easy way to find specific types of information in AOL's Travel channel is to use the Find button at the bottom of any screen. When you click it, you'll be able to scroll through an alphabetical list of all the channel's resources. If you want to browse through a category of information, click the Search by Topic tab. You then can choose from such categories as Travel Ideas, Destinations, Facts & Advice, Transportation & Lodging, Vacation Packages, and Travel Bargains.

# BOOKING TRAVEL ON AOL

Preview Travel is an online reservation system that lets you book flights through AOL. You can access the service by clicking the spinning earth icon in the Travel channel's Book It! area. Or you can use the keyword **reservations**.

If you're booking a flight, you also can make reservations for rental cars and hotels. At this writing, Preview Travel plans to enhance the system to make it possible for you to book cars and hotels independent of airline reservations.

The system is easy to use. It offers clear and simple instructions throughout. (It's similar to the process you used in the Microsoft Expedia site in Lesson 9, "Booking Travel Online.")

If you want to see how Preview Travel's reservation process works before you use it, click the New Users button in the upper right corner of Preview Travel's main screen (see Figure 25.2). Then select the Tutorial for New Users. It will walk you through the reservation process step-by-step.

Preview Travel also offers a vacation package service (keyword: vacations). It includes information on special deals and promotions. Both the reservation and vacation services also are available on the Web (**http://www.reservations.com** and **http://www.vacations.com**).

If you're an American Express card-member, you can use another online reservation system on AOL: Express Reservations (keyword: express res). It lets you book flights, rental cars, and hotels. Like Preview Travel, Express Reservations is an easy to use system that walks you through the process. If you have any problems, click the ? button in the lower right corner of the screen.

**FIGURE 25.2**   Preview Travel lets you make reservations through AOL.

# GAINING A TRAVELER'S ADVANTAGE

Travelers Advantage is an online travel club that promises special deals and travel savings, including a five percent cash bonus on eligible travel purchased through the club.

Members also can get special pre-negotiated prices on cruises and vacation packages, three hotel savings plans, car rental discounts, and a hotline that provides information on short-notice travel specials. Members can book travel online through Travelers Advantage Website (**http://www.travelersadvantage.com**).

You can sign up for a three-month trial membership with Travelers Advantage for $1. You'll be billed the full annual fee ($49 at this writing) unless you call 1-800-843-7777 to cancel your membership before the trial period ends.

Travelers Advantage also offers a full money-back guarantee if you're dissatisfied with your membership. For complete details about the club, use the keyword TA to access the area shown in Figure 25.3.

**FIGURE 25.3** Travelers Advantage is an online club that promises savings and special deals.

# MORE AOL TRAVEL RESOURCES

Here are notes on a few other features you can access through AOL's Travel channel. The keyword is listed in parentheses if it differs from the name of the feature.

 **TIP**   **Join AOL Newsgroups**   You can post messages to travel newsgroups through AOL. For more information, see Lesson 15, "Participating in Travel Newsgroups."

## TRAVEL GUIDES

- **Travel America...Online** (TAO) is a collection of official state and city visitors guide. You also can access America's Favorite Zoos and Aquariums, which provides general information on over eighty zoos, aquariums, and wildlife conservation parks. And you can search Ski America for profiles of ski resorts.

- **California Wine Country** (wine country) contains information on lodging, wine, wineries, current events, and relevant Web sites.

- **DineBase** (dine) reviews about 1,000 U.S. restaurants.

- **Destination Europe** offers country information, details on vacation packages, and online tools (currency and distance converters, for example).

- **Destination Florida** is an online guide to the sunshine state.

- **Lanier Bed & Breakfast Guide Online** (B&B) provides information on more than 14,000 B&Bs worldwide.

## TRANSPORTATION

- **AAA Online** (aaa) offers information on member benefits, destination details, and message boards for motorists.

- **Cruise Critic** provides unbiased reviews of more than 100 vessels, including cruise ships, sailboats, expedition vessels, river boats, freighters, and luxury hotel barges. You also can use an online program that will help you select a cruise.

- **InsideFlyer** calls itself "the world's authority on frequent flyer miles and points."

## GENERAL RESOURCES

- **Independent Traveler** (traveler) is "a community of travelers who enjoy the fun of planning their own trips and the adventure of independent travel." You can find information on bargains, tips, message boards, a travel library, chats, and an online travel book store.

- **Global Citizen** offers tips for business travelers.

- **Travel Corner** provides information on the U.S. and Canada as well as other countries, cities, and ports. You also will find a great deal of travel advice. For example, a feature called Ask Arnie lets you pose questions to a travel expert.

- **Family Travel Network** is, according to its creators, "the place where parents and kids can talk to other parents and kids and experts about the cool places to visit, hot deals, off-beat weekend activities, travel tips, resources and more."

- **Arthur Frommer's Secret Bargains** (frommer) lists travel deals in several categories (see Figure 25.4).

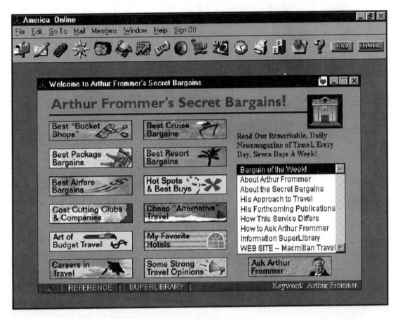

**FIGURE 25.4** Arthur Frommer, author of several travel guides, offers tips on dozens of deals.

In this lesson, you learned about travel resources on AOL. In the next lesson, you'll learn how to keep up with developments on the Internet.

# 26 LESSON

# KEEPING UP WITH THE INTERNET

*In this lesson, you'll learn about resources that can help you stay up-to-date on Internet developments.*

## TRACKING INTERNET NEWS

Trying to keep up with the Internet has been compared to trying to carry water in a sieve. As mentioned in the introduction to this book, new technologies seem to arrive daily. Web sites remodel their pages or disappear without warning. Trying to keep current on new companies, products, and services can overwhelm online users.

It can be especially challenging to identify the best online information sources. Technology has made it easy for anyone to become a publisher. With so much information available today, you need to find out where the information you're using comes from, how current it is, and how reliable it is.

One way to keep up with the Net is to monitor a Web site that provides news about information technologies. One such site is CNET's NEWS.COM (**http://www.news.com/**). It provides an excellent example of how the Web can be a powerful news medium. NEWS.COM's own staff updates the site at least three times every business day—in the morning, midday, and late afternoon. The staff posts breaking stories throughout the day.

On the Front Page (shown in part in Figure 26.1), you'll find headlines about high-tech; click them to get the full stories. Click the menu bars on the right of the screen to access news in such categories as The Net, Computing, and Intranets. Note that you also can search the site for news about specific topics. Just enter your keywords in the search box on the right of the screen.

**FIGURE 26.1**   CNET's NEWS.COM illustrates the Web's potential as a news medium.

As you scroll down the home page, you'll see more headlines and a Resources box in the left column. If you click the Search button in the box, you'll have more options than if you use the Search feature on the home page. For example, you'll be able to search a date range or browse stories by topics.

If you click the Get Newsletter button in the Resources box, you can sign up for a free service that delivers news and late-breaking bulletins to your e-mail box every business day. You can choose to receive the news in plain ASCII text or, if you read e-mail with Netscape Navigator or HoTMaiL, you may want to opt for HTML-enhanced dispatches.

If you register as a member (just click the button Join Now for Free near the top of the page, see Figure 26.1) you can sign up for customized news. Here's how:

1. Click the Custom News button in the Resource box.

2. On the next page, click the here link in the sentence "Click here to create your Custom News page."

3. The next page lets you select the type of news you want to receive when you visit the NEWS.COM site. In Option 1 (see Figure 26.2), select categories of interest by clicking checkboxes.

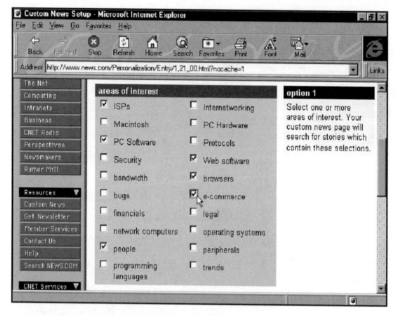

FIGURE 26.2    NEWS.COM lets you create your own customized Internet news page.

4. Scroll down the page until you see Option 2. It lets you enter terms in a search you want to run whenever you visit your custom news page. Note that you can use Boolean operators (for more information about them, see Lesson 5, "Searching the Web").

5. Option 3 lets you select the NEWS.COM departments you want to receive information from. Please note that if you select one or more departments, this option will override your areas of interest and keywords to deliver the most recent fifteen departmental stories.

6. Option 4 lets you set how far back Custom News should look for stories that match your profile.

7. After you've made your selections, click the Customize my news button at the bottom of the screen.

8. You now will see your custom news page. You can book-mark it in your Web browser to return to it and get up-dated articles in the future. You also can access it by clicking the Custom News button in the Resources box anytime you visit NEWS.COM's home page. You can change the Options you've made by clicking the link in the upper right-hand corner of your customized page.

## MORE INTERNET NEWS SOURCES

- MSNBC (**http://www.msnbc.com**), the joint venture between Microsoft and NBC news offers an excellent gen-eral news site. You often can find computer and Internet stories in the Scitech and Commerce sections.

- CNN Sci-Tech (**http://www.cnn.com/TECH/ index.html**) covers high-tech and general science topics.

- Computer News Daily (**http://www. computernewsdaily.com/**) is a service of The New York Times Syndicate.

- Internet Daily News (**http://www.tvpress.com/idn/ idnfp.htm**) offers information in such categories as law and politics, consulting and marketing, online job hunt-ing, and reviews of electronic publications.

- The Yahoo! Technology Summary (**http://www. yahoo.com/headlines/compute/**) offers Reuters headlines on computers, the Internet, online services, CD-ROMs, and multimedia topics.

- Yahoo! also offers links to more than forty other Net news sources. Go to **http://www.yahoo.com/** and select the categories News and Media, Technology, and then Daily.

- PointCast (**http://www.pointcast.com**) is a news service that automatically sends you the type of informa-tion you want when you want it. After your computer receives the news, the PointCast software will display it in a screen saver. The software is free, and it's available for both Windows and Macintosh users. Visit the PointCast site for complete details.

# USING ONLINE COMPUTER JOURNALS

PC World Online (**http://www.pcworld.com**) is a Web site sponsored by the popular computer journal. The Web site is popular, too; more than 50,000 people visit it every day.

You may want to go there to help you keep track of computer and Internet developments. The site is updated daily with news, reviews, and how-to articles.

Besides the online version of the magazine, the PC World Online Network includes several electronic publications that exist only on the Internet, including THE WEB Magazine (**http://www. webmagazine.com**), and NetscapeWorld (**http://www. netscapeworld.com**).

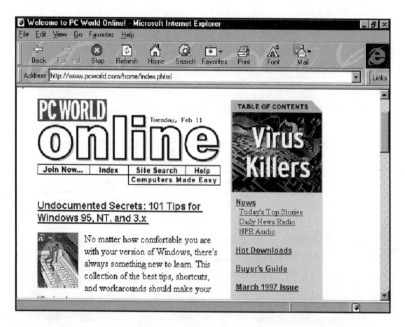

FIGURE 26.3    PC World Online is an electronic version of the popular publication — and a lot more.

PC World also offers TipWorld (**http://www.tipworld.com**). It will deliver "computer tips, news, and gossip" to your e-mail box every business day. You can select the type of information you want to receive by clicking boxes on the home page (shown in part in Figure 26.4).

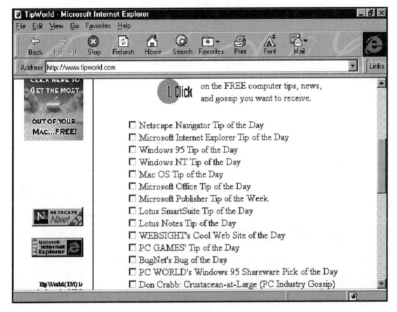

**FIGURE 26.4** TipWorld automatically delivers computer advice and news to your e-mail address.

## OTHER ONLINE INTERNET JOURNALS

The following sites are the Web versions of Internet journals that help you explore various subjects on the Internet. Many of these sites include reviews of other Web sites. Most of the sites post at least selected articles online.

- Internet World **http://www.internetworld.com**

- Link Up **http://www.infotoday.com/lu/lunew.htm**

- The Net **http://www.thenet-usa.com/**

- NetGuide  **http://techweb.cmp.com/ng/home/**
- Online Access  **http://www.onlineaccess.com/**
- Web Week  **http://www.webweek.com/**
- Wired  **http://www.wired.com/**
- Yahoo! Internet Life  **http://www.yil.com/**

## GENERAL COMPUTER JOURNALS

These are the Web sites of several popular computer journals. They often cover Internet topics as well as general computer developments.

- *PC Computing*  **http://www.zdnet.com/pccomp/**
- *PC Magazine*  **http://www.pcmag.com**
- *PC Week*  **http://www.pcweek.com**
- *MacUser*  **http://www.zdnet.com/macuser/**
- *MacWEEK*  **http://www.macweek.com/**
- *Macworld*  **http://www.macworld.com/index.shtml**

To find the online addresses of more computer and Internet magazines, use the URL **http://www.yahoo.com**. Then select the following categories: Business and Economy, Products and Services, Magazines, Computers.

# PRINTED INTERNET DIRECTORIES

There are many printed directories that call themselves Internet Yellow Pages or something similar. For example, the New Riders' Official World Wide Web Yellow Pages covers more than 8,000 sites.

The book includes a CD-ROM with a fully searchable electronic edition. It also contains a unique system of navigational guides, an exhaustive index, and numerous cross references. You can order the book online from Macmillan Publishing's Web site (**http://www.mcp.com/nrp/wwwyp/index.html**). You also can access a Web version of the yellow pages at that address.

Another useful printed resource is Que's Mega Web Directory. It contains more than 18,000 site listings sorted by topic. The complete listings also are available on a CD-ROM that includes a search utility you can use with the book or on the Internet. You can sign up for an annual subscription that will provide up-to-date information monthly.

To keep up with the newest online travel resources, you also should use the search engines explained in Lesson 5, "Searching the Web," and the directories in Lesson 6, "Using Electronic Transportation and Travel Directories." Sometimes the best way to keep up with the Internet is simply to keep traveling on it.

# INDEX

## X-Z